Praise for "JOURNEY to FREEDOM"

Charlotte Marky's story is bigger than one poor girl's rocky road to America. It's the story of World War II, of communism's grip on much of Europe, of death and tears and the power of faith and the heart to overcome almost anything. It's not something you will soon forget.

—Terry Pluto, Cleveland Plain Dealer

After the first few pages I became entranced by Charlotte's story. The description of her childhood during Hungary's dark days of Nazi occupation and communist rule both captured and revolted me. At times, it was painful to read about the horrors Charlotte and her family endured. Her stark style of writing—simple, sometimes rough in texture—somehow seems appropriate for the somber circumstances, much as a film in black and white can be, if done right, more powerful than in color. I understood, through Charlotte's eyes, the hopelessness, and emptiness of life without freedom. Her emotions seemed to be held in check as she describes the details of her arduous journey to freedom—physical freedom at least. It is only at the point of her encounter with Christ and subsequent *spiritual* freedom that her heart is exposed—for she was finally safe in the Savior's arms.

—Pastor Jim Colledge, Hudson Community Chapel

Many times one picks up a book and within the first three chapters finds it predictable. There is nothing predictable about this story of the heart that winds its way through your very core with deep love of family. Somehow, that love enables them to endure through the unimaginable. It is a story of being lost and being led by the mighty hand of God to a place of safety, love, and blessing.

—Katherine Kuehl, Assisting Pastor
Holy Trinity Anglican Church, Hudson, Ohio

JOURNEY
to
FREEDOM

A Young Girl's Story

of

World War II and Communism,

of

Revolution and Escape,

and the

Power of Faith to Overcome

JOURNEY

to

FREEDOM

by

CHARLOTTE J. MARKY

TATE PUBLISHING & *Enterprises*

Published by Tate Publishing & Enterprises, LLC
127 E. Trade Center Terrace | Mustang, Oklahoma 73064 USA
1.888.361.9473 | www.tatepublishing.com

Tate Publishing is committed to excellence in the publishing industry. The company reflects the philosophy established by the founders, based on Psalms 68:11,
"The Lord gave the word and great was the company of those who published it."

Book design copyright © 2007 by Tate Publishing, LLC. All rights reserved.
Cover design by Leah LeFlore
Interior design by Lindsay B. Behrens

Published in the United States of America

ISBN: 78-1-60247-847-3
1. Inspiration   2. Motivational   3. Biography & Autobiography
07.10.26

DEDICATION

This book is dedicated to the late Rev. C.C. Thomas and his wife, Marjorie, co-founders of the Haven of Rest Ministries of Akron, Ohio. Their integrity, humility, love, and compassion for all people left an indelible impression on my life.

To the Rev. Curtis Thomas and his wife, Eileen, they expanded the ministry begun by Curt's parents. Their continued commitment and dedication to serving and meeting the physical and spiritual needs of those who are touched by this ministry is an inspiration of seeing faith in action.

The Haven of Rest Ministries trusts God, depends upon God, prays to God for provision, then walks by faith, touching lives and transforming people through the power of Jesus Christ.

It is my desire to honor God with my life for His faithfulness and unfailing love: ten percent of everything I earn from this book will be donated to the Haven of Rest Ministries of Akron, Ohio.

ACKNOWLEDGEMENT

To those who have helped and encouraged me I want to express my sincere thanks. My precious family and dear friends your prayers, encouragement and gracious gift made all this possible.

Late Pastor A. Harold Arrington, faithful servant of Jesus Christ, thank you for reflecting Him by your kind and gracious spirit and genuine friendship.

Anita, Valerie, and Tim, my beloved children, you are God's gracious gift, and give me much joy.

Curt and Eileen Thomas, your lives reflect Jesus through your servant spirit, thank you for your faithful prayers.

Peggy Colyer, dear friend, thank you for your prayers and daily encouragement.

Clarissa Thomas, dear young friend and "adopted" daughter, thank you for your assistance with the computer, and cheering me on to keep writing.

Katie Kuehl, Andrea Crow, and Tracy Mock, thank you for taking time from your busy schedules to proofread the rough drafts.

Darron C. Thomas, thank you for your generosity, and prayers.

Above all, I thank my God for His unfailing love and faithfulness.

CONTENTS

PART 4

PART 5

FOREWORD

I am honored to write the Foreword for this book, *Journey to Freedom* written by my friend, Charlotte Marky. My wife and I have known her since 1960 when she was nineteen years of age.

The book that you now hold in your hands is a remarkable story of God's saving grace. For years, missionaries have traveled around the world, faithfully proclaiming the Gospel so that people in various cultures would hear and accept God's salvation. However, this fascinating story is just the opposite. Charlotte Marky, a fifteen-year-old teenager left her family and her homeland of Hungary and journeyed thousands of miles to a new culture, America, where she met Jesus, the Savior of the world.

The heart of this story reveals there is a significant difference between being religious and being a Christian. As the Associate Director of the Haven of Rest Rescue Mission in Akron, Ohio, I remember the Saturday night in December 1960 that Charlotte attended a service at the rescue mission. After hearing the compelling testimonies of changed lives, she responded to the invitation at the close of the service and was led to Christ by my mother, Marjorie Thomas. At that very moment in time, Charlotte experienced ultimate freedom.

As you accompany Charlotte Marky on her life's journey through this book, you will experience excitement, fear, anger, tears, and triumph. But more importantly, if you have not done so already, may you experience personally the joy of knowing the truth, because "the truth will set you free" John 8:32b.

-Rev. Curtis Thomas, Jr.
Executive Director Emeritus
Haven of Rest Ministries
Akron, Ohio

The
Journey
began
in
Hungary

PART 1

WHERE IT ALL BEGAN

Kislang, a small farming town, is located in the section of Hungary known as Transdanubia, "beyond the Danube." Transdanubia is the region west of the Danube River, the longest river in Central Europe, which divides Hungary in half. While Hungary is located in central Europe, the way of life of the Transdanubian people was strongly influenced by Western European culture. Kislang was a community with a stable social order and a strong work ethic. The people were friendly, deeply loyal to family and community, self-reliant and hard working. It was a peaceful little town with a population of about 1,000. Most of the people were farmers, and agriculture was the backbone of the economy. Four "mom and pop" general stores supplied a variety of goods, and everything the residents of Kislang needed was available in town. There were shoemakers to custom make shoes and boots from the leather of your choice and tailors to sew clothing to your specification. These tradesmen were truly artists. The blacksmith's shop was a busy place; he repaired a variety of farm machinery, fixed wagon wheels, and shoed horses. The yard at the grain mill was always crowded, heavy wagons loaded down with grain ready to be ground into flour, farina for cooked cereal, corn and other grains for feeding the animals. Although most of the woman in town did their own baking, the town had a wonderful bakery that supplied the local restaurant and stores with delicious breads, crusty rolls, and croissants.

The streets, laid out in a grid, allotted one acre of land to each house. Lots were narrow and long, with houses neighborly and close to each other. An attractive picket or iron fence enclosed each residence for privacy. Built fifteen feet from the street, the houses were all very similar, a long ranch-style with tile roofs and a porch running the entire length of the house. The main entrance to the home was accessible only by entering through the front gate, and then, through a courtyard. Picturesque flower gardens in the front yard of each house expressed the creativity of the mistress inside. These perennial flower gardens were a beauty to behold. Varieties of plants in a rainbow of colors arrayed the gardens: pansies with their little faces along with the snowdrops, tiny purple violets, yellow daffodils, and red tulips heralded the arrival of spring.

Other garden favorites were the delicate pink bleeding heart with arching sprays of dangling pink heart shaped flowers, and little pink and red primroses with their delightful fragrance, and the lily-of-the valley with clusters of soft white bells. The lilac bushes and the locust trees that lined our street filled the air with a heady fragrance. There was no public transportation in town, so everyone walked or rode bicycles. It was a pleasure to walk down the streets and enjoy the vibrant display of flowers along the way.

As the seasons changed so did the flowers in the garden. Later in spring, the peonies in shades of pink, white, and red with large fragrant flowers provided a spectacular display. The pure white lily with its sweet fragrance was in full bloom by Easter. All summer, the gardens throughout the community dazzled with a display of color and fragrance that delighted the senses. Almost every gardener cultivated beautiful old-fashioned pink, red, and yellow rose bushes. Dahlias, with their kaleidoscope of color throughout the summer, gave endless opportunities to harvest armfuls of flowers for bouquets. Elegant gladiolus, white daisies with yellow centers, snapdragons, zinnias, asters, phlox and other flowers too numerous to mention overflowed the gardens. Hollyhocks made tiny dolls for little girls to play with. Flowerpots bursting with geraniums lined the windowsills. Grandmother's favorite flower was the stock, in shades of white, yellow, pink, and purple. Mother always gathered flowers to bring indoors. Flowers were food for the soul and a delight to the heart.

Beyond the living quarters lay the barnyard with a variety of barns and stables for all the animals, followed by sheds and outbuildings for farm machinery, and barns to protect the hay and other food stored for the animals. To keep the animals from roaming, the barnyard was enclosed with a fence. Next was about half an acre of vegetable gardens where the family produced all the food they would need to can and preserve to last through the long winter months. The remainder of their property was outside the city limits. Endless acres of farmlands surrounded each town. Every day during the growing season, the farmers would hitch their horses to wagons and made their way to their land to plow, plant, cultivate and finally to harvest their crops.

North of town, beyond Spirit Lake, lay the vineyards and fruit orchards. At the right time each fall, the families gathered and harvested the grapes and made wine. Hard working farmers found an occasion to celebrate, and they would always have an annual harvest festival with dancing at the community center in town.

Spirit Lake held an endless fascination for small children. On several occasions, flames of fire would burn on the surface of the lake. There was a scientific explanation for that phenomenon, but we children liked our version much better. Spirit Lake was about one kilometer from the town's cemetery. With our imaginations running wild, the flames, we were positive, were ghosts escaping from the cemetery.

The Town Hall and the Police Station were located in the center of town on Main Street. All legal matters were taken care of there. The three school buildings were also downtown and all children were required to complete and graduate from eighth grade. Those desiring higher education moved to a city of their choice. When not in his office, the doctor would ride his bicycle, making house calls, attending to the medical needs of the families, delivering their babies, and vaccinating their children. The owner of the pharmacy was a pharmacist and an herbalist; the shelves and cabinets in his pharmacy displayed an assortment of bottles filled with herbal extracts and tinctures. The room resembled a chemist's laboratory. He mixed and concocted the medications for all the prescriptions the doctor ordered. Just about everyone had an herb garden where the many variety of herbs were cultivated for medicinal purposes. Living in a farming community, the local veterinarian was always busy treating all the domesticated animals and pets.

To minister to the spiritual needs of the community, there were two churches in town, a Catholic and a Protestant, each with their own cemeteries. The cemeteries were side by side. The only difference was at the entrance to the Catholic cemetery, over the gate, the inscription stated *We Shall Rise*. I puzzled and wondered, "If they rise, where will they go? What will happen to the Protestants if they don't rise?"

The Community Center housed a small library, and a large auditorium with a stage. Plays, concerts, graduation ceremonies and monthly dances, brought the community together for fun and relaxation. On Saturday and Sunday afternoons and evenings, a special feature entertained the moviegoers. There were two pubs with a limited menu, since most people cooked at home, but there was no limit on the other liquid refreshment they provided.

Kislang was ideally located. Less than an hour's drive northeast was the beautiful and ancient city of Szekesfehervar. The name of the city means the "Seat of the White Castle," a reference not only to the white stone of the buildings, but also to its function as a center of Royal power. White was the chosen and distinguishing color of the Hungarian Kings. Szekesfehervar was one of the most historic sites of Hungary, having been for centuries the coronation and burial place of kings.

Lake Balaton was about an hour's drive northwest. It was Hungary's most popular summer resort, with beautiful beaches. On a clear summer day, the water sparkled and danced with blue and white lights. At other times, the color was a wonderful combination of blue, gray, and silver. The color and the light changed with the seasons. Shallow Lake Balaton could have sudden and violent storms. It was a favorite fresh water fishing lake with a large variety of fish. The northern shores of the lake were excellent for growing grapes and deservedly well known for the white wines of the region. Budapest, the capital city of Hungary, was only about two hours away northeast.

Kislang was an ideal place to raise a family. Everything the community needed was available and they had easy access to many other larger cities and recreational areas. In this small town, Francis and Julianna Csepregi lived with their extended families. It was here their families owned a considerable amount of property.

Julianna came from a family with eight children. Her father was the town's treasurer for many years. They were a respected family in the community. Francis came from a blended family of ten children. His father had been widowed with six children to raise. He moved to Kislang where he met Katalin, who was a widow with one daughter. They married and had three children of their own, two of whom died shortly after birth, only Francis survived. Four of the five children from his first marriage had immigrated to the United States in the early 1900's before Francis was born.

Marton, from his father's first marriage, and Julianna, from his mother's first marriage, were the only siblings he had left in Hungary after the death of his parents.

When Francis and Julianna were married in 1940, they moved into the paternal Csepregi ancestral home. They shared this home with Marton who was also a business partner with Francis. Marton's young bride had died of tuberculosis and he never remarried. She was the love of his life.

It was to this home of Francis and Julianna on October 20, 1941, that the doctor and the mid-wife came to assist with the delivery of a baby. The young mother had a raging fever and the doctor worked diligently to save her life while the midwife attended to the tiny little baby girl. This little baby was the young father's pride and joy. She was so tiny that she fit snugly into his large and capable hands. Lovingly he cared for her while his young wife was fighting for her life.

They named their little girl Charlotte Julia. I was that little baby girl.

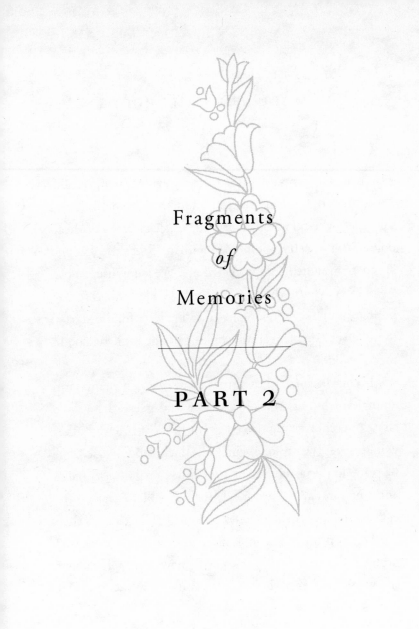

Fragments

of

Memories

PART 2

MEMORIES OF CHILDHOOD

My parents often said I was a strong willed, happy child. I was my father's daughter and I adored him and followed him everywhere I could. Our Puli, a special breed of sheep dog, was my self-appointed guardian. Since we had no sheep, he watched and protected me. We were inseparable. I would crawl after him or lay down beside him. One day, pulling myself up by hanging onto his long fur, he started to walk, very slowly, as I was walking beside him. He taught me to walk!

Living in small agricultural town, we had many farm animals including chickens, ducks, and geese. I loved to chase the chickens and feed them. Every spring, mother would save twenty-one chicken, duck, and goose eggs to place under a mother hen, or duck, or goose to hatch and thus provide future meals for our table. After all the eggs were hatched, she would give the babies back to their mother to protect and look after. The mothers were very protective of their little ones. Whenever she felt danger, she would gather all her little ones under her wings. One day, my mother brought into the kitchen a small basket of baby ducklings to keep warm until the rest of them were hatched. She sat the basket on a table and covered it with a soft cloth. She was busy working and did not notice what was happening. Curiosity got the best of me; I wanted to play with the baby ducklings. As time passed, she realized how quiet it was. She came to check and saw me with the basket of ducklings. Looking at Mother, little fingers on my lips, I said, "Shh, be quiet, they are sleeping." She was horrified to see that they were all dead! Loving them, and squeezing too hard as I laid them down to sleep, I had loved them to death.

She took them, looked at me, and said they were dead and would not wake up. Punishment was not necessary, as broken hearted, I cried. Later that day, she told Father. He held me close as I told him the sad little story about loving the soft little baby ducklings, putting them to sleep and Mommy saying they were dead and would never wake up. Father gently said, "Little treasure, you are not to hold tightly onto anything that you love." I would never forget my first experience with death, even as a young two-year-old. Sadly, it would not be long before I would see even more horrifying deaths.

Mommy had good news to share, one day I would have a baby brother or a sister. What were babies? I did not understand and soon forgot all about it.

I was too little to know that Hitler's war machine was moving across Europe, and very soon it would change our lives forever.

WAR THROUGH THE EYES OF A CHILD

The threat of war was becoming more of a reality each day. It was no longer happening in far-away lands. Our little family had to face the painful reality of it when my beloved Father was called up to serve in the military. Mother was expecting. Her joy and anticipation was overshadowed by the harsh reality that she would have to face those future days without her husband. Separation is always painful, even more so in a time of war. It took months to hear any news from the front and when we received it, it was old news. Alone, mother gave birth to a son, Francis Stephen, on November 28, 1943. When his tiny son came into the world, Father was fighting somewhere on the Russian front.

As the rumors of battles came closer and closer to our town, Mother and Uncle Marton boxed up some of our valuable possessions, including the family silver and china, important documents and other items that Mother hoped to save. They dug deep holes in several places on our property and buried the boxes. During those days, I seldom asked questions. I just watched and observed all that was going on around me. My beloved Father was gone and Mother was very busy taking care of my baby brother and preparing the best she could for the worst possible situation. I was bewildered and lonely.

One day while playing in the front yard of our house, I unlocked the gate and walked out to the sidewalk. I was happily skipping down the street when my play was interrupted by a very strange sound. I stopped to watch; there were trucks, jeeps, and tanks rolling down the street, roaring with noise. I was afraid, yet I could not move. I flattened myself against the chain link fence, my tiny hands clutched the links behind me, as I watched this terrifying sight passing before me. After the endless parade of vehicles moved on and turned the corner, there followed a long endless line of foot soldiers. Mother realized I was not in the yard. She came looking and found me flattened against the fence, shaking. As she scooped me up, I wrapped my little arms around her neck and she carried me home. This was the start of the German occupation. I was told that we did not have to be afraid of the soldiers, because they were our "friends." But they were not "friends" to all Hungarians, because some of our friends and neighbors had to wear a yellow star on their clothing, just because they were Jews. The Germans came and took them away. We never saw them again. Only one man, a friend of my father, returned after the war. He told my parents that his wife and our neighbors were sent to the "ovens" in the concentration camp. I was too young to understand the horror of it.

Shortly after the arrival of the German soldiers, we could hear planes flying overhead and the deafening noise of bombs exploding. Bright lights lit up the dark night, followed by more bombings. Mother would grab Frankie and we would run to the fruit-cellar under the summer kitchen just across our yard. She had prepared it ahead of time so we would have water, food, extra clothing, and blankets to keep us comfortable, no matter how long we would have to stay down there.

Several of the German officers set up their headquarters in the front half of our house. They allowed us to use our small bedroom and the kitchen. Father had a short wave radio, which had very good reception. They chose to add that to their collection of all types of equipment they used. Mother kept both of us very close to her side, and under careful watch. We still had our farm animals and Mother was able to cook and bake for us. The German officers always asked if Mother had enough to share with them. They took their meals in privacy, seldom left their equipment, and always listened to their radios.

We could hear the fighting around us escalating, with the Germans and Russians in a tug of war over Hungary. By war's end, this whole region endured seven advances and retreats of the German and Russian army. We spent more and more time in the cellar. By this time, Aunt Elizabeth and our two cousins came to stay with us, along with some of our neighbors. We had a large sturdy cellar built solidly with bricks and a reinforced roof. The bombings were getting closer and closer. We were all afraid. The women were praying. The only people left behind were women, children, and old people. The men had been called up to serve in the military.

The fighting intensified. We did not dare to leave the cellar thus we had no news. Suddenly the door was kicked open and harsh, loud voices were ordering us to come out. Our worst fears became reality. The Germans had retreated and the Russians invaded our town. A wave of destruction, as was never seen before, followed in their wake. They looted, destroyed, and raped along the way. We hardly recognized our yard, with carcasses of dead animals strewn about the front porch. The Russians demanded that the women cook for them. They were starving and had no supply of food. They existed on whatever they pillaged as they ransacked the countryside. When the food was only partially cooked, they grabbed the pots and pans and devoured everything in sight. The soldiers cut up some of our furniture and used it as firewood. They stole everything they could lay their hands on. Some of the soldiers had as many as ten to twelve wristwatches on their arms.

The soldiers had lice. They would take off their shirts and throw them at Mother to iron them, so the hot iron would kill the lice. Unfortunately, we all got the dreaded lice and we children suffered very much. Mother washed our clothes with lye soap, scrubbed, and cleaned. It was a futile effort and eventually the day came when Aunt Elizabeth and Mother had to cut off our long hair and shave our heads. I remember watching big tears rolling down my Aunt's face as she cut off little Elizabeth's beautiful blond curls. They did what they had to do—the best they could. We were at war. A brutal enemy who had no regard for life or property occupied us.

The war raged on. Heavy fighting started up once again. It rained and rained. The roads turned into mud. Most of the tanks and armored vehicles were stuck deeply in the solid mire. This time the Russians were pulling out. In order to move their equipment, they stole all the horses in the neighborhood and hitched them to the tanks to pull them out of the mud. We never saw our horses again.

Some of the soldiers came back, tearing into our yard, to take whatever else they wanted. Loyal, little Puli furiously barked trying to defend her property and the people she loved. Mother tried in vain to call her. She was giving the best her little body had to protect us. One of the soldiers kicked her and shot her. Mother was holding Frankie in one arm and with the other hand, she had a tight grip on my arm, keeping me from running to Puli, as she lay motionless. I cried and cried and could not be comforted.

The Russians were retreating and the Germans were returning. The battle was fierce; both sides were fighting to win. Caught in between the two lines we literally had no place to go to escape the fighting. Down in the cellar, we were anxiously waiting for the outcome. As the first line of German soldiers reached our town, they ordered us to evacuate. Mother, Uncle Marton, Aunt Elizabeth, along with several of our neighbors, gathered as much of our few remaining belongings as we could carry, and started walking toward Veszprem, an old historical town north of Lake Balaton. That part of Hungary was still under German occupation. We had heard we would be safer there.

Our little band of refugees included: Uncle Marton, Mother, Frankie and me; Aunt Elizabeth, her son and daughter; our neighbors, Elizabeth and her son Alex; Helen with her two boys and her elderly parents. Because Grandparents Labadi and other aunts and cousins lived in a different part of town, they had to evacuate in another direction, thus our families became separated.

We began the long hazardous journey of sixty-five kilometers to Veszprem. All the adults were loaded down with whatever clothing and food they were able to gather. It was a hard and miserable trip. Mother carried baby Frankie in one arm and a basket of food in the other. I walked close to her side, trying to keep up, but my little legs would get tired and then Uncle Marton would carry me too. I loved him very much; he was always a part of our family. Yet he was fifty-six years old and he would get tired. He had been a valiant soldier in the First World War and was awarded with many decorations for his outstanding military service. He also received twenty-five acres of land from the government for his heroic service; this was the land that my family lived upon.

Time and distance had no meaning. We struggled from village to village, resting, and finding shelter along the way to Veszprem. A small convoy of trucks full of German soldiers caught up with us. One driver stopped and offered the women, with small children, a ride in the small space in the back of the truck. Uncle Marton insisted we accept. Mother and Aunt Elizabeth, with the four of us children, climbed in. A heavy tarp covered something that we could not see. Soon Mother and Auntie discovered they were sitting on the bodies of dead German soldiers. They were horrified. Mother knocked on the back of the window, motioning to the driver that she wanted to get off. She could not bear the thought of sitting on dead bodies.

The soldier answered back to her, "Madam, you don't have to be afraid of the dead. They will not hurt you; however, if you want off, I will stop and let you down." Hastily we stepped down from the truck and, of course, found ourselves separated from the rest of our group. As always, Mother was carrying baby Frankie in one arm and I climbed on her back, wrapping my arms around her neck. She had a basket of food in the other hand as we continued on our journey. Laden as she was we could not walk very fast, we were soon caught in a bombing raid. Bombs were falling all around us, in front of us and behind us. The noise and the flying dirt were unbearable. Mother was praying for our safety, and if that was not possible, that we would all die together. This was her constant prayer during the war. Frantic with fear, Mother fled, dodging large holes, flying debris, until finally, we reached a small village and found shelter with an elderly couple. We stayed there for a while until we heard that it was safe to return to our home.

Not knowing where else to go, Mother and Aunt Elizabeth, with four of us children returned home. As people returned, we heard bits and pieces of news about the rest of our extended families. Aunt Frances, Mother's oldest sister, was badly wounded with flying shrapnel and was being cared for in a make shift hospital. Fortunately, Grandfather and Grandmother Labadi were with her at the time. That was the last news we would hear for a very long time; we never heard any more news about their whereabouts until after the war. Thankfully, she survived, but there were several pieces of shrapnel in her body that could not be removed. Over the years, she suffered greatly with it.

After returning to Kislang, we realized that the rumors we heard of it being safe were false. Despite the bombings and the ransacking, we still had our house. However, the Russians were back, and we feared for our lives. They were like the locust, devoured every bit of food they could lay their hands on: they even killed horses and ate them. We had no place left to hide anything from them. They always demanded food, even when we had nothing left to give.

Young girls were not safe from them they would run and hide. Some disguised themselves as old woman and walked stooped over, so the soldiers would not notice them. Mother and Aunt Elizabeth discovered that the Russians hated to hear children cry, so whenever the soldiers came around and demanded they cook for them, or iron the lice on their clothes, they would pinch us, and we would scream and cry. Then the soldiers would leave disgusted and angry, throwing or breaking things.

For the fourth time, the fighting shifted. The Germans advanced and the Russians retreated. Uncle Marton returned home with a wagon and a horse and we set off to Veszprem once again. As we approached Aracs, a small village, other families trying to reach safety also joined us. A small plane flew overhead, rained tear gas down on us. It was horrible. It burned our eyes and we could not stop crying. Days later, we were still suffering from the effects of it. The plane did not have any identifying marks; no one understood who would do such a horrible thing to defenseless children and women.

In Aracs, we found shelter with another family. It was crowded; they already housed two other families, then Helen and her two sons and her parents joined us. We shared very small quarters in this house, nevertheless we were grateful for the shelter and the relative safety from fighting. We cooked our food on a wood burning stove and it kept us warm. Good firewood was scarce. Thus it happened one day Mother picked up baby Frankie, held my hand, and walked outside to gather firewood around the edge of town. We found an open field with many broken tree limbs and she worked quickly to gather a bundle. The noise of an airplane broke the silence. Nearby stood an old ruin, so she hurried us across the open field, to hide in the shadow of the wall, until she could determine which type of a plane it was. Too late, the pilot had already noticed us and opened fire. Reaching the wall, Mother clutched us close and we huddled together, pressed against the wall. The plane circled overhead, raining bullets down on us. It was flying so low, we could see the pilot. Mother watched the plane; when it flew on one side of the wall, we would rush to the other side to hide behind what little shelter the wall provided. The pilot continued to shoot at us. This went on for a long time; we lost count of how many times we fled from one side to the other. The plane kept circling and we kept running from one side of the wall to the other. It seemed that the plane could not continue in this circling pattern for much longer. He made a wider circle and Mother took advantage of the opportunity. With her lungs heaving from exertion and fright, she grabbed us close, and then she ran so fast my small feet barely touched the ground as she propelled us across the open field to the shelter of the nearest house. The plane circled for two hours over the little village before he finally left and we were able to return safely to our house. Again, we never knew if this plane was Russian, German, or Hungarian.

The Russian army was on the move once again. They were getting too close for comfort, so Mother and Aunt Elizabeth gathered our few belongings, and we resumed our evacuation to Veszprem. It was slow going for two women on foot carrying small children. We finally reached a small village named Also Ors, and we sought refuge. Several families joined us, including Helen and her two sons; it was wonderful to see them again.

The German army occupied Also Ors. They usually left civilians alone; at least they did not terrorize us as the Russians had. Hunger was our constant companion. We had no food, let alone necessary nourishment for babies. We do not know how or why it happened, but one day a German officer delivered to our house some milk powder and farina, food for babies and children. The women were grateful, thanking him for his unexpected kindness. He smiled and said, "I am a father of a little girl like that one." Pointing to me, he asked Mother if he could hold me. She was reluctant, but finally agreed. He gently picked me up and he held me close and kissed my little face as tears were flowing down his own. As he was leaving, he told Mother he hoped that someone would show kindness to his family and his little girl. For several weeks, he would bring whatever he could to feed us. Always he would ask if he could hold me. I came to know this kind soldier and I would scamper to him and put my little arms around his neck.

Frequently, bright lights lit up the night and thunderous explosions would echo in my ears. Bombs were falling all around us. The Russians were advancing again. We could not travel fast enough or far enough to outrun the war. After a long night of bombings, there was an eerie silence. Anxiously we waited for news of the battle, which side was the victor? We did not have long to wait. Two angry Russian soldiers kicked the door down and ordered everyone out to stand in the front yard. Earlier that morning, Aunt Elizabeth and one of our neighbors took their children up to the attic hoping to see what had happened during the night. Thus, they had a perfect view of what transpired below. The Russians forced us to line up: Mother, Baby Frankie, myself; Helen, her two boys, her parents, and the two women who owned the house.

Mother was holding one-year-old Frankie; I was three years old, clinging to her leg, terrified. Staring at the two soldiers, I saw one had a bloody white cloth wrapped around his head and there was blood dripping down the side of his face. He had a black thing in his hands. (Years later I learned that it was a revolver.) The other soldier had a dark green uniform and long boots on his feet. He held a big gun in his hands. He was screaming at us in Russian. He held up his hand, counting on his finger, "One…two…" just as he was to say "three," a Russian jeep carrying officers drove by. In an instant, they saw what was about to take place and shouted to the soldiers. The soldiers turned, saw their rank, lowered their guns, and left the yard. Numb, Mother sank to her knees, embracing us tightly for dear life. We were sobbing our hearts out. Shortly, Aunt Elizabeth with her children came running to us, hugging us, crying with relief. We were safe for the moment.

Mother knew we must leave Also Ors quickly. So we repacked our few belongings and we slowly continued our way to Veszprem. Veszprem is a beautiful old historical town just north of Lake Balaton. While kings were crowned in Szekesfehervar, the Seat of the White Castle, queens were crowned in Veszprem, the Queen's City. Finally, we were here, and it was in the Queen's City where we sought refuge from the ravages of war.

One day Mother surprised us. She had found a little girl named Edith, age seven, and her brother Nicholas, age five; they were lost and separated from their grandparents. Mother, with her tender loving heart, adopted those two children and kept them, watched over and protected them. They lived with us for two years after the war. It was a tremendous responsibility for her. Mother was a petite young woman but she was strong and fearless in protecting her children. In town after town, mother left messages with the local residents informed them of our whereabouts in case the parents or grandparents were trying to locate the children.

We lived this nightmare for almost two years. I have no recollection of anything pleasant or fun, only fear, ugliness, and horror. My nights were filled with nightmares of dead bodies, and especially of the "bloody one." The shootings, bombings, and endless days in cellars were taking their toll. We were always hungry. Mother cried because she had nothing to feed us. We were weak from hunger. On and on the war continued. Would it ever end?

At last, the unbelievable news reached us, the Allies had defeated the Germans, and the war had ended. As a small child, I could not understand the historical significance of the Allies victory. The bombing had stopped, that is what I remembered. War demands a high price. Everywhere we looked, we could see destruction, devastation, and ruin.

Once an outgoing and happy child, I became quiet and withdrawn. I did not complain or cry. I wanted to go home. I wanted my beloved Father.

GOING HOME

We were a long way from home and how would we return? Weak from hunger and exhaustion, we were in no condition to walk back to Kislang. Yet, even while separated, we had someone searching for us, and amazingly he found us. One day uncle Marton arrived in a wagon pulled by an old horse. He had come to take us home. We were so happy to see him. Home meant seeing Father again, with no more separations, living in our house and playing in our yard.

Every child should have an Uncle Marton in her life. He was kind and thoughtful. He was the only one of the six children of Grandfather Csepregi's first marriage who remained in Hungary and did not immigrate to America. His oldest sister, Anna, and her husband sailed for America in the early 1900s, leaving two daughters behind in the care of the grandparents until they could send for them. Unfortunately, they both died shortly after they arrived in America leaving the girls orphans. As the years went by, Grandfather and Grandmother Csepregi also died. The girls remained in the care of Uncle Marton. Eventually they married and started families of their own. Their husbands were also drafted into the army. They, too, were alone to manage the best they could. Since our families did not live in the same area, Uncle Marton would make sure that we were safe, and then he would go and try to find out how they were getting along. Under severe hardship and great personal risk to himself, he would walk from town to town to make sure that we were all safe and cared for. He took his responsibility as the patriarch of the family very seriously. We knew that he loved us very much.

In the spring of 1945, we were on our way home. The old horse struggled as he labored to pull the wagon, even though it was practically empty. We had no possessions, everything we owned we left behind when we had to evacuate. Along the way, Mother saw a young horse feeding in the field. She was able to catch this horse and Uncle Marton hitched it to the wagon next to the old horse. She was untrained and had never been harnessed to a wagon. Yet, next to the old horse, she quickly learned to pull as a team as we walked our way home. Sadly enough the old horse died along the way. He was pulling so hard and his poor body was just skin and bones. It was a wonder that he even survived the war. He just collapsed and fell, his pitiful, starved body lying motionless on the ground. My little mind was numb, remembering the baby ducklings and little Puli. I knew this poor horse would never wake up. It was up to the young inexperienced horse to take us home and that she did.

We arrived in Kislang on Resurrection Sunday in 1945; resurrection that wonderful reminder of new life. Little did we realize what was awaiting us. Fire damaged part of our house and the remaining half was unbelievably filthy. Most of our furniture had been chopped up for firewood. The Russians had kept the animals in the bedrooms and the stench was unbearable. Our yard was littered with dirt and debris. We were stunned, our senses overwhelmed. We were hoping to find our home; instead, we found destruction and the horrible reminder of war. Everything we had to leave behind was gone, looted and stolen. The gardens, the flowers, and the trees were trampled and cut down. This place did not resemble our home. The home I longed to return to, a place where I once felt safe and happy, was destroyed. Worst of all, Father was not there waiting for us. Oh, how I needed to see him! I wanted to be held in his strong arms and be comforted. As an adult, I wonder how my dear tiny mother had the strength to go on. Her loss was unbelievable. Her hopes and dreams for a happy life with her husband and little family were shattered so soon after her marriage. She was now alone to protect her two small children, not even knowing if her husband was alive and coming home to this devastation and total loss. Now as a mother myself, I wonder how she felt, all this by age twenty-three. Whatever she felt, we, her children and Edith and Nicholas, were her primary concern. She had backbreaking work to do, and lots of it.

Mother and Aunt Elizabeth set about to bring order out of the horrendous chaos; we needed a home. Only a few of the town's people had made it back yet. We were eager to meet with them, to learn whatever news we could about the whereabouts of relatives, husbands and friends. Our eagerness soon faded into sadness and disappointment, as time after time, no one knew the whereabouts of Father. Always hoping, we never gave up, but as the months became years, the pain of loneliness became more difficult to bear. Where was he? What had happened to him? No words could explain how I felt. Though I could not talk about it to anyone, fears and hopes were buried deep in my heart.

One day Mother decided to take us to her parents' home to see what she could find. Our shortcut crossed through the back gardens, and then led to a main path, which led to grandfather's house. We walked down the path careful to avoid a huge hole, made by a bomb, in our neighbor's garden. Many of the locust trees that lined the path looked as if someone had wielded a giant axe and hacked them to kindling. One locust tree somehow survived there were no flowers on it yet, but tiny new leaves were budding, a reminder of spring, new life, and a new beginning. Something was hanging from one of the limbs; I took off running, curious to see it. I was too quick for Mother to catch me. There, on the tree limb, was hanging a badly decaying form of a man. A tag pinned to his clothing read, "this is the fate of all deserters." My eyes were riveted on that body. Standing sided by side we stood stunned, staring, then Mother reached for my hand and said, "Let's go home." She told several of the neighbors, and they removed the body and buried it. Later, other bodies were found and buried, some right along the roadside, with crosses marking their graves.

Even though the war was over, we had to be very careful. Many innocent people were hurt from the unexploded ammunition lying around. Mother watched us constantly, we did not survive the war, only to be hurt by a grenade hidden in the yard. The clean up process was painstaking and extensive; it was a long time before our community was safe once again.

One by one, our extended family members were returning home. Grandfather and Grandmother Labadi arrived home with Aunt Frances and her family. Such joy, we were so happy to see them. Grandfather was very sick with pneumonia and there was no doctor nearby to help him. The town doctor and his family had perished in the "ovens." The nearest place for medical help was in Budapest, but he was very sick and travel was difficult at that time.

I loved my Grandfather. He was a kind and gentle man and he loved his family very much, especially Grandmother. Mother told us that Grandfather's parents were prosperous farmers and they wanted their son to marry the daughter of another prosperous farmer. The two families intended to arrange the marriage of their children, a very common practice in those days. Grandfather would not hear of it; he was in love with a petite young woman. Her family was not as well to do, but it did not make any difference to Grandfather. He loved Julia, and if she would accept his proposal, she was the only girl for him. Grandfather was firm in his resolve to marry Julia and eventually his parents reluctantly agreed.

Their union was blessed with eight children, three boys and five girls. Grandfather treated Julia with much respect and tenderness; it was obvious they loved each other very much. Growing older, I hoped that one day I would meet someone who would love me as much as he loved his Julia.

Slowly, Grandfather recovered his strength and I was allowed to visit him. Taking the shortcut, Mother would accompany me to the garden path until we reached my Grandparent's garden, only then would she let me walk by myself. Sitting by his bedside, holding his hand, we were there for each other. In reality, he was there for me. The gentle touch of his hands and his tender words of affection were a healing balm to his brokenhearted grandchild. When he was strong enough to walk, he would walk with me to the garden path. He knew I was afraid to pass by the locust tree. Horrifying memories of childhood heal very slowly. Surrounded by a loving family, the assurance of their love worked magic in the healing process. Even though the times were hard and difficult, it was wonderful to know that I was loved. Their love gave me the security I needed even in the hardest and ugliest times of my life.

Aunt Elizabeth's husband, Uncle Kalman, also arrived home. They were so happy. He was a very talented carpenter and furniture maker with several apprentices working for him. As the years went by, they were able to rebuild their house. Eventually, a few at a time, our aunts, uncles, and cousins returned home. But where was Father? Mother asked everyone who came through our town if they knew of his whereabouts. Without words the anguish and pain in her eyes told us that not one of the returning soldiers had news him.

Through some business contacts, Uncle Marton heard of a returning soldier, in a nearby town, who knew Father. He decided to visit this soldier to find out for himself; he had to be sure that this man knew his brother. We had not heard from Father for over two years. The only news we had was a note written on the bark of a paper birch letting Mother know he was in Russia and that he loved her very much. What had happened since then? At long last, we had news of Father! Uncle Marton learned that Father had been wounded in Russia. His company was on assignment to locate the Russian forces and report their movements to his main unit. He was assigned to communications and he used Morse code to send messages. Scouting out ahead seven of his company were on the east side of the river. On the other side of the river, the main unit was waiting for their signal to cross. The surrounding area of the Don River was swamp filled with quicksand and extremely dangerous. This crossing was too hazardous for the main unit and he messaged the unit in time, thus saving the lives of many of their comrades. While trying to return to the main unit, all seven of them, carrying their equipment, were walking single file on a ridge when a sniper opened fire, killing the first man, and wounding the remaining six. Father was shot through the wrist and the bullet grazed his side but fortunately did not penetrate his chest. His friend and schoolmate was seriously wounded. Father would not leave him behind, so he carried him on his back, only to find out that he died along the way. Sadly, they never made it to safety. Deep in the heart of Russia, they were captured and imprisoned.

As best the soldier knew, Father was in a prison camp somewhere in Russia, if he was still alive. Uncle Marton, a seasoned soldier himself from World War I, did not believe his brother could be alive after all this time in a prisoner of war camp. He had painful news to bring to his hopeful sister-in-law. It was with a heavy heart that he delivered his message.

Mother was so small, five feet, two inches, and thin from the many years of starvation and walking from place to place to protect her children. She overcame pain and suffering, and nerve-wracking experiences. She remained strong even in the face of losing everything she owned. Finding her house in shambles, she rolled up her sleeves and went to work to rebuild, hoping for a reunion with her husband, hoping to start anew, to bring beauty from ashes. She never gave up hoping that one day her husband would return. This news was devastating to her. She could not hide her tears, they were rolling down her face; she gently sobbed, her heart was breaking.

Mother and Uncle Marton took inventory of what remained of our belongings. Our immediate and greatest need was food. Ours was a farming community; we depended on the food we grew. Farmers could not grow anything during the war. In a neighboring village, Uncle Marton purchased two sacks of wheat. He brought it to the mill and had it ground into flour. He heard that a cow was for sale in Lovas, a village about fifty kilometers from Kislang. He walked several days and led that cow back so we could have milk.

Family, friends, and neighbors were helping each other plant vegetables and secure food supplies. Nineteen forty-six came and went, and Mother was working very hard to provide for us. Hardly a day went by that we did not talk about our Father. Where was he? Was he alive? During this time, Edith and Nicholas were still part of our family. I was sure they could not help but wonder if they would ever see their parents again.

During the winter of 1946 and 1947, Grandfather Labadi became very sick. Depravations during the war and his bout with pneumonia had compromised his health. We knew treatments at the hospital in Budapest offered the only hope. The family had no choice even though the trip was difficult.

After the examination, the doctor assured him that roentgen ray treatment would help him. The hospital overflowed with sick people and lacked sufficient nursing staff. The doctor instructed a nurse to take Grandfather down to the roentgen room and apply the treatment to his chest for a few minutes. The nurse set him up, turned on the equipment, and then left to attend to someone else. The family waited and waited for him. Finally, after an hour or so, they looked for the nurse. She was very busy and forgot about Grandfather, and had left the machine unattended for over an hour. She was honest and did tell the doctor, unfortunately, there was nothing more he could do. With irreparable damage done, without hope of recovery, the family brought him home.

Months passed and Grandfather noticed evenly spaced red dots on his chest and back. In a short time, those red dots became holes and then the holes oozed liquid. He was getting weaker and weaker, and was soon confined to bed. Visiting him every day, sitting by his bed, holding his thin hands and stroking them was all I could do. Talking was difficult for him. Words were not important; being there and holding his hands was all I needed. The desire to see him was so strong I would even walk the garden path alone. Approaching the locust tree I would run as fast as my little legs could take me until I made it to Grandfather's garden. I do not know why I always chose this shortcut when I could easily have walked down the street without fear to visit them.

FATHER COMES HOME

June of 1947 was a memorable day for our family. Frankie and I were playing in our yard when we heard the familiar sound of a horse drawn wagon coming to a stop in front of our house. Looking up from our play, I started to run toward the gate, as the man stepping down from the wagon was running to me…"Daddy! Daddy! Daddy!" was all I could say as he scooped me up in his arms, collapsing to his knees and holding me tightly. Small, thin arms wrapped tightly around his neck clinging onto him, never ever letting go. Frankie watching us, inched closer and timidly hugged this man, the Father he could not remember. He tugged at my arm, at the back of Father's neck asking, "Saci, is he my Daddy too?" There we were, the three of us, holding onto each other and sobbing with joy when Mother and Uncle Marton found us a few minutes later.

After three and a half years, Father was finally home. His six feet, two inch frame resembled a walking skeleton, weak from starvation and weighing only forty-seven kilograms. He was suffering from malaria, digestive disorders, and numerous other health issues. His burning desire to see his family again kept him alive.

I was almost six years old and my brother was four. Our childhood memories were only of war, separation, and hardship. Indescribable fears and horrors were buried deep in my heart. Things that I could never voice in daylight, only my nightmares would bring them to the surface. Now my beloved Father was home and our family was together. At last, happiness was seeping into my heart.

Father was very sick. Mother did everything possible to nurse him back to health. To regain his health, he needed nutritious meals and proper medical attention, things that she could not provide. Post war Hungary was very poor, thus Father's recovery took a long time. Two and a half years of depravation in prison camps had taken their toll on his body.

Nineteen hundred forty-seven was a year full of life changing events. Father's presence had a transforming affect on all of us. Spending time with him, seeing him every day, talking with him and hugging him calmed my fears. At night when Mother tucked me in, I no longer spent anxious hours wondering where he was or if he would ever come home; I could sleep peacefully with only an occasional nightmare.

We had no electricity. Yes, we had the fixtures hanging from the ceiling and the walls, but there was no power. We used kerosene lamps that Mother would hang over our kitchen table. Every room in our house had a lamp that we would light as needed. We carried water from the well for our daily needs and did not have the convenience of indoor plumbing.

I never realized as a child just how poor we were and how much our parents lost during the war or how it hurt them that they could not give us more than the barest necessities of life. We had very few material goods, yet when a beggar or a gypsy came to our house and asked for food they were invited in and my parents would share whatever they had. Father was a sensitive and thoughtful man. He believed in the dignity of all men, treated everyone with respect and courtesy, and expected his children to do likewise. Because of their example, I learned very early in life the virtues of kindness and generosity. They could not give us material things, but they gave the best gift that any child could have, they gave of themselves, their time, and attention. Little did I know how being cherished and loved unconditionally would sustain me in the coming years.

As my beloved Father's health was improving, my dear Grandfather's health was deteriorating. Grandmother took care of him faithfully. She was beside him everyday; no one could make her leave. She did everything to take care of his physical needs. She washed the homemade dressings that had to be changed so frequently and cut up more and more of the sheets to apply to his chest. She frequently bathed him and kept his bed clean.

Grandmother Julia was a homemaker with artistic abilities. She was a petite and slender woman with a gentle disposition. All her children and grandchildren loved her. Her clothes were a work of art, she designed and sewed beautiful linen and cotton dresses, with gorgeous embroidered fine linen blouses, bodices, aprons and kerchiefs. Embroidered and monogrammed linen beddings, wall hangings, tablecloths, and napkins decorated her rooms. Crocheted lace tablecloths and doilies covered her dressers and small end tables. She knitted beautiful sweaters for her family. All five of her girls learned the gentle art of homemaking, and they were all accomplished and talented in that area. The walls of her home and porch were painted and stenciled with delicate floral patterns. Her gardens displayed a large variety of flowers. Every time I spent a night at my Grandparents' home, I felt like a little princess surrounded by her beautiful creation and I always enjoyed her excellent cooking.

Grandmother loved Grandfather very much. Nursing him and caring for all his needs was a service of love. Being a regular visitor in their home, sitting beside Grandfather while holding his hand, I saw the gentle love that was so evident between them. Life held so many mysteries that I could not understand, but being surrounded by an atmosphere of love in my grandparents and parents' home was a healing balm for my troubled heart.

Something was terribly wrong. I overheard whisperings of death. Grandfather was dying. Fear with its icy fingers gripped my heart. "Death," what is it? Death appeared as an invisible yet very real being. It was something that caused the little ducklings, once so sweet, soft and cuddly, to become hard and lifeless. "Death" caused all those bodies to become ugly and terrifying. "Death" was something I feared.

Edith, age nine, and Nicholas, age seven, were still part of our family. Nicholas was a kind and nice playmate but Edith kept to herself, and many times, she was mean. She, too, heard about Grandfather dying, and when she was in a particularly nasty mood, she taunted that "Death" was coming to take Grandfather away. "It is not true, it is not true," I screamed and ran to my bed crying. Sobbing, I would fall asleep from exhaustion. Edith had a talent for drawing. All the adults who saw her art said so. I do not know why she did it, but she drew a picture of her idea of "Death" and propped up the drawing on a chair next to my bed, so when I awoke I could not miss seeing it. It was a black hooded figure with a skull for a face. When I saw this horrible picture of death, I fled. Seeing me leave, she walked in and retrieved the picture, thus hiding her bad behavior.

Mother made every effort to locate their parents or grandparents. Finally, one day their grandparents came and they were reunited. They were very grateful to Mother for protecting them and keeping them safe all these years. Just before the war ended, their parents had settled in Germany, and eventually Edith and Nicholas would join them. I was glad to see Edith go.

Father was improving. He was up, walking about and helping around the house. We were all very happy to see him looking better.

Life was moving on. School was to reopen in September. I was almost six years old. Judith, my best friend, and I spent lots of time playing together and making plans for school. We had no idea what school was like but we were looking forward to it. We did not have a normal childhood, so events that would have been a routine part of ordinary life were all new to us.

Next, the citizens of our little town concentrated their energies in rebuilding and restoring public buildings. Most of our homes were livable for the time being but now the schools and churches needed our attention. The church had always been the center of our town. Now it lay in rubble. The members of the church held a meeting and decided that it was time to rebuild. The building project required many months and long hours of volunteer labor. Finally, the building inside and out was completed. The entire congregation had a day of worship celebration. The completion of the church building gave a glimmer of hope for a new beginning to the community of people who had lost so much and suffered so greatly.

WHEN GRANDFATHER DIED

A deeply felt sadness settled over our community, Grandfather was dying. He was well known and respected member of the church and the town treasurer for many years. The entire community rallied behind Grandmother, encouraging and supporting her. Daily friends and neighbors would stop by to pray and visit. Someone from the family was always present to make sure that Grandmother had all the help she needed. Every moment I had, I wanted to be with Grandfather. Unexpectedly, Cousin Elizabeth asked me, "Aren't you afraid he will die while you are there?" I had never thought about that. Grandfather could no longer take liquids; he was slowly starving to death. I heard Grandmother say to the family one day that Grandfather was seeing something in the corner of the bedroom, a shadowy figure that made him uncomfortable. She called the priest to pray for him. He rested better after the priest's visit. From that day forward, she kept the lamp burning in his room until his death. Even with the burning lamp, every night, the shadowy figure moved closer to his bed and then one day, Grandfather told Grandmother that the shadowy figure was standing at the foot of his bed. On that day Grandfather died!

His entire family and extended family gathered that evening at the home for the wake. They prayed, cried, prayed, and cried more. There were so many people in the house. According to customs, Grandfather's body was transferred to the front room and laid out on the bed. They placed lit candles on the four corners of the bed. The family went in and out, paying their last respects. No one noticed as I quietly entered the room to see Grandfather for myself. I needed a step stool to reach the top of the high old fashioned bed I used to sleep in when I spent the night, so I just climbed up, and stood on the top step looking down at Grandfather's motionless form, with tears rolling down my face. I was not afraid of being in this dark room with flickering candlelight; I loved my Grandfather with all the love my six-year-old heart could hold. From a very young age I was always analyzing, observing, and keeping all these things buried deep inside. I carefully touched his hand, the hand I loved to hold. It was cold. I was troubled. Where did "Death" take Grandfather? I was afraid of "Death." "Death" was a mystery.

I left the room and returned to the kitchen; no one even noticed I was gone. There were so many people in the room, all praying, and crying. Crawling under the kitchen table, I sat there and listened to the adults pray. This is where my Mommy and Daddy found me and then they took me home.

According to customs, the burial must take place on the third day. Godfather Kalman, who was the town's carpenter, was also the funeral director. He custom made all the caskets and conducted the funeral services. On the third day, the extended family gathered at the family home. Grandfather's body lay in the casket lined with funeral cloths and a pillow for his head. They placed a prayer book and a crucifix in his hands. The family said their final good-byes before Godfather Kalman came and nailed the coffin shut. The family, along with all the mourners, gathered in the front yard praying and singing, but not even the singing could drown out the sound of pounding nails into the coffin. Then the pallbearers carried the casket outside and placed it on a special table draped with funeral cloth. The priest started the memorial service for the dead. After praying, singing, sprinkling of the holy water over the casket and making the sign of the cross, he waved the incense burner over the casket. The incense of the dead had an unforgettable fragrance; it lingered in the air, a painful reminder of loss.

The funeral procession to the cemetery was my very first experience of such formal ceremony of death. The coffin was placed in an elaborate black hearse drawn by horses. The driver and Godfather Kalman, holding the temporary wooden cross with the name of the deceased, were the only ones riding in the hearse. The rest of the funeral procession was following on foot. According to tradition, the entire town attended the funeral service.

The grave had been dug and prepared ahead of time in the family plot. The pallbearers placed the casket over two strong poles stretched across the grave. As the priest was conducting the graveside service, people were praying and singing, while four men lowered the casket into the grave. I was standing in front of Mother, looking down into the grave where Grandfather's body was placed.

I saw and heard his casket reach the bottom, then they pulled the ropes out. People began throwing flowers on the casket along with handfuls of dirt. It sounded horrible. Soon they were shoveling the dirt on the top of the casket. I wanted to blot out the sound. "Death" had taken Grandfather down into this black hole, covered him up with dirt, and I would never see him again. Finally, it was over. All the flowers the family and friends carried were covering his grave. Reluctantly, taking Mother's hand, we began the long walk home, leaving Grandfather behind, all alone.

No one realized the heartbreak and pain I felt. I could not talk about it and many nights I cried myself to sleep. Years later Mother said I had mourned Grandfather's death longer than anyone they could remember. More than anything else in my short life, "Death" had left a permanent terrifying imprint on my life. "Death" was an enemy, an unseen enemy. He robbed you of people you loved and took them to a deep black hole, and nobody could do anything to stop him. I feared "Death."

SCHOOLS REOPENED

Without electricity, there were no phones, no radios, and no contact with the outside world. Our source of communication was the town crier. He would walk up and down the streets, beating his drum to the tune of a march. Arriving at a designated area, he would beat the last tunes of his march to a grand finale, gathering all the people in the surrounding neighborhood to come and listen as he read the current news. He would do this once or twice a day depending on the importance of the news. It was during such an event we heard the news that school would open in September and all school age children had to be enrolled for classes. Some of the older children had already missed one to two years of school. It was an exciting time for parents and children alike.

The start of school was the beginning of new experiences. For the first time, our lives became very structured. We went to school Monday through Saturday from eight a.m. to one p.m. We had our little backpacks to carry our schoolbooks, notebooks, and pencils. We walked to school and along the way met up with our classmates.

Children had to stand at attention whenever a teacher walked into our classroom and we could not sit down until the teacher indicated to do so. We all had assigned seats for the school year. Talking or whispering was forbidden in the classroom. The principal would walk down the hall and ring an old-fashioned bell to announce the break after each hour. At one o'clock, we were dismissed from school, with our homework assignment for the next day.

RELIGION CLASSES

Shortly after the opening of our school, our religious training would begin. The local priest was our teacher. I liked religion classes; they were full of mysteries and things unknown to me. Yes, I heard my Mother and others pray during the troubled years of war, but I did not know the God to whom they prayed. It seemed very important to them, that was all I knew. I heard them pray when my Grandfather died. Somehow, I sensed that the God they were praying to could not be seen, but was very real and somehow controlled everything in life. Actually, He was someone to be feared. I thought He lived in our church building because everyone was very quiet when they entered, dipped their fingers in holy water, knelt, and made the sign of the cross on their chests.

Our classes were one hour long. The priest told us stories about creation and stories about people who lived a long time ago. People like Adam and Eve, our first parents, who sinned. Since we were all born with that original sin we needed to be christened as babies. He told us repeatedly, it is very important for us to learn and obey all the rules of the church.

The Bible, a book I had never seen, had many wonderful stories. It was a very important book and it was holy, and only the priest could read it. He told us about Noah and the ark that he built, and stories about Cain who killed his brother Abel. Even though I did not understand their significance, I liked the stories from the Bible, they were interesting.

We learned more than stories; we must learn rules and prayers too. We had to learn the commandments, because if we broke them there were very serious consequences to follow. During these times, my heart was filled with fear. Would I be able to remember all those rules? What were the serious consequences? This God that everybody prayed to so earnestly must be very hard to please. Deep down I felt that no matter how hard I tried, I probably could never please Him. These rules were something you obeyed and never questioned. I just pondered them in my heart.

Our church building was simple, compared to some of the great cathedrals, but to this little girl it held many mysteries. The paintings were of people who lived a long time ago and there were statues of saints and people who must have been very good and never broke any of those commandments. There were several altars to kneel and pray before, with many different saints to intercede for every need. An offering box was in front of each altar. Those praying there always put money in to ensure that their prayers would be answered. There were many prayers to memorize from our prayer book for special occasions. Going to school, learning to read and write, and study math seemed so much easier than learning all the do's and don'ts of religion class.

FIRST CHRISTMAS

The first Christmas I remember was very special. Father was home and we actually had a small tree that mysteriously appeared on Christmas Eve in time to celebrate the birth of the Christ Child. It was a simple tree, decorated with cookies and walnuts. The post war years were very hard. We were all very poor and our entire nation was poor. As a little girl, I did not know the difference, as I did not even realize that we were poor. I had my Daddy, my Mommy, Frankie, Uncle Marton, and all my friends; I was very happy.

In religion class, we heard the Christmas story, so I was looking forward to going to church on Christmas Eve with my family, especially to see the Nativity Scene. It was a very cold winter night and we were all bundled in our warmest clothes. All our friends and neighbors were walking to church that night, carrying lanterns to light our way. The church looked very pretty in candlelight. As was customary, all young children stood in front of the pews, very close to the altar. Only the adults could sit and the teenagers stood behind the pews. Everyone knew exactly where their place was and made their way quietly there. It was very cold inside the church, but as soon as the organ started to play and everyone joined in singing the beautiful Christmas carols, we forgot how cold it was. I was lost in the wonder of the Christmas story.

After the service we all filed by the Nativity Scene. It was beautiful. The life size statues looked so real: Mary in a blue gown, Joseph standing close by her with all the shepherds, sheep, and a donkey. In the center was the most beautiful little baby Jesus, lying on a manger of hay with his little arms outstretched. I could hardly wait for my turn as I stood in wonder and awe at the lovely sight. Just like all the others before me, I knelt and leaned over and kissed his tiny feet. I was only six years old and did not understand the significance of His birth. That night, as I was holding my Father's hand and walking home, watching the beautiful starlit sky and the Milky Way with its millions of stars, they seemed so close I felt I could reach up and touch them. For a brief moment in time, all the fears, the pain and misery of my small life seemed far away in the afterglow of that Christmas night.

FRIENDS

Judith and I were best friends. We started and finished first grade together, and now summer was here. Two new families moved into our neighborhood and both families had girls our own age. Helen and her family moved in next door and Annie and her family moved next door to Judith. We were all neighbors and it did not take long to get acquainted and then to become inseparable. Judith was an only child. Helen and Annie each had an older brother, and Annie also had a younger brother. We spent the long summer days playing tag, hide-and-seek and many other games that we would invent.

One day Helen's father told us that the "stork" was going to bring a baby to their house and we should be watching for it. We sat down by the well, watching the sky looking for the "stork." Time was passing by and still no "stork." We had a serious discussion of just how a "stork" looked and how would it carry a baby. Late in the afternoon, Helen's father found us and announced that the "stork" had arrived and left a baby brother. We all looked at each other in disbelief. How could that have happened? We were watching all day. The only birds we ever saw were pigeons. We were so disappointed at missing the "stork" that we showed very little enthusiasm to see the new baby.

All too soon, summer was over and we were preparing for second grade. All four of us would be in the same grade and in the same classroom. Receiving our seat assignments, Annie was assigned the seat next to me and Helen and Judith were sitting side by side. What fun!

The beginning of school meant religion classes would start again. This year we would be preparing for our confirmation. This was a very important time in our life and we spent most of our class time studying for it. We received a rosary and we learned how to use it. We memorized more prayers and received a prayer book. We had to learn so many things. I was more earnest in memorizing than in understanding what I memorized. I was so afraid of the consequences, if by chance I would forget some of it.

We learned about God, that He was exalted and that He knew everything, even what we were thinking. He saw everything. He was very strict, and we had to learn all these rules and sacraments so we could please Him. Jesus, the sweet little baby in the manger, grew up. We could see His trial and death illustrated in the fourteen stations carved from stone, which decorated the walls of our church. On special occasions, the priest would take us for a walk in the churchyard to a grove of trees that formed a pretty alley where we could see a repetition of the fourteen stations in a lovely garden setting. He himself tended this garden. Although it was in a garden setting, the statues depicted something horrible. Jesus was beaten and nailed to a cross. He died on that cross. It was sad to walk in that grove. Here was "Death" again. There were so many crosses and all were reminders of "Death": there was the cross in front of our church, the one at the end of Main Street, one at the entrance to the cemetery, and many over graves, and on our rosaries. Crosses and Death—I pondered the connection.

The Ten Commandments was our next lesson and that began our study of sin. There were so many sins. I knew about some of them. Mommy told me I must obey her, be a good girl, and not fight with my brother. I had to share and not be selfish. There were so many more sins that I had never heard about; we had a little book that listed them. Some of them were "cardinal sins" and if we ever committed one of them, we would surely go to hell. We learned about confession, which was telling all our sins to the priest, so he would forgive us and tell us what prayers we had to say in front of the altar.

We learned about heaven, hell, and purgatory. As a child of seven and eight, I knew that only very good people, like saints and martyrs, ever went to heaven. All the bad people went to hell and all those who had committed cardinal sins, since they could never be forgiven, went to hell. All the rest would end up in purgatory. Their only hope of ever getting out of there was to have someone say prayers for them, or offer special mass services for the dead, so they eventually could get out. Nobody knew just how long this would take.

We went to church every Sunday and I would go to confessions every time and tell the priest all the sins I could remember. The last sin I would tell would be "I lied," because I did not know if I remembered to confess everything. Then he would tell me to pray at the altar so many prayers and I would be forgiven. The scene portrayed on that altar was terrifying to a young child. Moreover, it was a large group of statues, their very size was intimidating. At the top was Mary sitting high on her throne with baby Jesus in her arms. He had a tiny crown on his head and His little arms reaching out. Under Mary's throne, encircling her throne were flames of fire reaching upward but never touching the throne. People were chained together in the flames, in agony raising their arms and beseeching Mary and Baby Jesus. I knelt at that altar and said my prayers. I remained kneeling, staring at the statues, especially the people in the flames. I knew deep in my heart that I would never go to heaven and I hoped that I would never commit any of the unpardonable sins. I was sure I would stay forever in purgatory.

Even at that young age, I realized that my dear Grandmother, who was at church all the time and said her prayers faithfully, would probably be dead by that time, so she would not be able to pray for me. My parents would be dead. There would be no one left to pray for me or serve mass and therefore, I would remain in purgatory for all eternity. There were two very real, but invisible beings, that I was afraid of, God and Death.

Our lessons continued with so many rules to remember. I felt sorry for Judith. Her parents were divorced and her mother remarried; since divorce was a cardinal sin, her parents would end up in hell. That troubled me. Annie's father was a member of the Reformed church and that was bad. We were forbidden to enter that church or we would surely go to hell. What would happen to her family? Helen was the lucky one. Her aunt was a nun, she knew all the rules and kept them, and her aunt would never let any of her family forget any of them.

Finally, we were ready for our confirmation ceremony. The entire class passed the test. We were very relieved and looked forward to the ceremony. We all had to wear white dresses. We choose a friend or family member who was a devout member of the church to stand with us. We also received a new name. Maria was the new name my confirmation mother gave me, and I liked that name. I received a prayer book with my new name written on the inside cover as Charlotte Julia Maria.

RISE OF COMMUNISM

The first day of third grade introduced some startling events into our lives. Along with these changes came unease and fear. As we entered our classroom, we were surprised to see all the familiar emblems of our nation, dear to all Hungarians, replaced with the pictures of Lenin, Stalin, and Rakosi, our Premier. The red flag of Russia replaced the Hungarian flag, and the coat of arms was replaced with the hammer and the sickle. Even though most parents shielded their children from the political changes in our nation, it was evident even to us that the events taking place would change our lives forever.

Religion classes were abolished and the church doors closed. We could not attend church; it was against the law. Our new teacher informed us that religion was the "opiate of the people." As an eight-year-old, I did not understand its meaning, but this I knew: religion was now forbidden. There would be no more stories from the Bible. I could not practice the sacraments. What would happen to the sins I committed? To Whom could I confess them?

The "young pioneers" meetings replaced religion classes. We had to wear a red scarf around our neck, symbolizing our allegiance to communism, which we were told would usher in Utopia. Day after day, we were reminded of the glories of communism. Our country would be purged from all those who oppressed the people. The Russian language was introduced into the curriculum. Daily we encountered changes in our classroom. We had new teachers and they were dedicated to transforming us into the ideal communists of the future.

These changes affected our daily lives outside the classroom. We were not allowed to use the name of God or refer to God in any way. Even such a little thing as how we greeted people was changed, instead of the traditional greeting, we had to say "Forward." This was our affirmation that we were putting the old ways behind us, and embracing the new ideology. Stalin, our big brother, was watching us and there would be serious consequences if we disobeyed. The names of our special holidays changed. Christmas Day became "Evergreen Day," and then it was removed from the calendar. While they could change the name of that special day, they could never erase the memory of that first Christmas day I celebrated with my family. On Resurrection Sunday, we remembered "spring and new life, baby bunnies, chickens and ducklings." Our city streets, named after Hungarian patriots, heroes, and former Kings, were renamed with Russian names and founders of communism, such as Marx and Engels. The Hungarian coat of arms and flag were removed from all public buildings and replaced with the red star and the Russian red flag.

It was very real to all Hungarians that the Communists were in charge. They used a variety of methods to teach us that this new way of life would eventually deliver the entire world from the corruption of capitalism and the warmongering West. They would ask questions about our parents and our friends. Did we know anyone who was against this new order?

As a child, I did not understand what "communism" meant. Our teachers declared that it would liberate people from oppression and everyone would share all things alike. There would be no rich or poor class of people. Everything was to be divided and shared equally among all the citizens of the land. It sounded good in the classroom, but we were all so desperately poor, barely recovering from the ravages of war. What was there to divide? Large segments of the country lay in rubble, and electricity had not been restored in the small towns and villages. We had no radios or outside contact with the rest of the world. Only some progress had been made in the reconstruction of the major cities.

The newspaper called *Free People* was delivered to every household. Filled with communist propaganda, it was the only news the government wanted us to hear. We read about the "5-Year-Plan" and the "10-Year-Plan," which promised the progress we would be making under the guidance of communism. In 1947, The Worker's Party enacted a Three-Year-Plan, an attempt to put the country on its feet quickly. The party announced a plan to collectivize the land, and introduced it in 1948. To accomplish this new "Utopia," the first order was to steal the possessions of those people who owned property, businesses, or land for they were said to have "oppressed" the people. They were denounced as "kulak" the enemies of the state. At first, they were given the option to willingly sign over their property to the state and join the new order of "collectives" owning all things in common. If they refused, they were imprisoned or deported, never to be seen again. Fear and terror reigned over our small town. One by one, our neighbors disappeared during the night. Stalin was a living symbol of terror. He caused millions of men and women to sleep in fear, half expecting his knock on the door.

The power of AVH (The Hungarian Secret Police) and its scope of operation increased. A network of informants betrayed the dissenters and kept the state informed. These domestic purges continued well into the 1950s. No one knew who these informants were, therefore, neighbor could not trust neighbor. Children, during classroom discussions, often innocently said something that would send their parents to slave labor camps and thus their children became the wards of the state. My parents, as most parents, never discussed anything in front of us. What we did not know, we could not tell. In a small town, even children realize that people were missing. The parents of some our classmates disappeared overnight. Although I was young, I still realized that something terrible was happening. What we learned in the classroom contradicted what we experienced in real life. The reality was the educated, the professional and the business class did not embrace communism. They had to be eliminated and a new breed of people to be raised up.

My dear Uncle Marton, a decorated soldier of World War I, was given property as a reward for his heroism. A kind man, he was now considered a "kulak," an enemy of the state. One day several men from the AVH without warning suddenly appeared, arrested him, and imprisoned him for six months to convince him to voluntarily sign over his land to the collectives, the land that they had already taken without his signature. Terrible fear gripped my very soul. What would happen to Uncle Marton? He was not an enemy of anyone. What would happen to all our friends?

What would happen to my Mother and Father? Could they be taken away also? This new philosophy, this new idea called "communism" which promised so much in theory, as it was explained in the classroom, brought with it fear, terror and torture in real life. Even as a young child, ten, eleven years of age, I realized that there was something very wrong at the core of this thing called "communism" if it had to eliminate a large segment of society who were good people, to accomplish their desired end. The spread of communism drastically changed our lives during the years of 1949 to 1956. The new order must be established, society had to be made compliant, if not willingly, then by force.

The AVH issued an order; all firearms had to be turned in to the Police Station. It was now illegal to own firearms. The possession of any type of gun was punishable by immediate arrest and possible deportation to Russia. To ensure that the citizens complied, the AVH made a house-to-house search, ransacking entire houses, every nook and cranny. They ordered us out of the house as they literally tore it apart. When they were satisfied that they could not find anything, they left. We had so few earthly possessions, we had lost so much during the war, and now what little we had was scattered all over the floor.

Even though the houses and gardens had barely recovered from the war, both were cherished even more by the owner. The majority of our town's people still had not signed over their business or land to the communist party voluntarily. The midnight knocks on the door and the disappearance of neighbors continued. Fear became a way of life. Uncle Marton was still in prison.

One evening, Mother went over to Aunt Elizabeth's to help her make a featherbed. Frankie and I were doing our homework when someone knocked on our door. Father answered the door and some men asked him to step outside. He closed the door behind him and left with them. We were in the bedroom studying and did not know what happened. It was late in the evening when Mother returned and wanted to know where Father was. We told her that he went outside when some men came to the door and he had not returned. The expression on her face was one of fear, of anger and of determination. She forbid us to leave the house, and locked the door behind her, she left. It was then that we realized Father had disappeared.

Mother, like an avenging angel, was running down the dark streets to the Town Hall and to the police headquarters. She was determined to find out what had happened to her husband. The Town Hall was dark, but finding the front door unlocked, she flung the door open and ran inside. In the hallway, she encountered one of our neighbors, who had turned communist. She screamed at him, "Joe, where is my husband?" He was so startled seeing her there, he just pointed. That was all she needed. She flung the door open, and there, before her eyes, was her beloved husband, strapped to an iron bed by his hands and feet, being badly beaten. She shouted at the top of her lungs, "Stop it!" The man froze, his arms raised high, ready to deliver another blow to Father's back with his club. There were several other men in the room. Looking into their faces, she recognized them as she demanded, "Untie him!"

Calling each communist traitor by name, she rebuked all of them, "You know my husband, he helped every one of you when you had nothing to eat and nowhere to turn. He gave you jobs; you sat at his table and ate his food. You also know he does not own any property or land, all of that was given to his brother, who at this time is rotting somewhere in one of your filthy prisons."

Somebody was untying Father. Staring at the naked, bleeding, and bruised body of her husband, she whispered, "Come Francis, let's go home." She reached down to help him stand up, covered him with some of his clothes, and led him out of the building. Not until standing together in the silent street did she realize just what she did. She felt sick, her knees were shaking, as they clung to each other and painfully walked home in the darkness.

My brother and I watched solemnly as she put our Father to bed. He was very badly beaten. His frail body, already weakened by his many months of suffering in a prisoner of war camp, complicated his recovery. As she sat at his bedside, the enormity of what she did dawned on her and she sobbed. What would have happened if they had imprisoned both of them? What would have happened to her children? Years later, Father told us how his "magnificent angel of rescue" flew to his aid. His Julia, his five feet, two inches, probably not weighing all of one hundred pounds wife, taking on a roomful of evil men to save his life. Little prepared for the life she lived, my Mother, a courageous young woman with the heart of a lioness, protected her little family during the horrible years of war, its aftermath, and during the scourge of communism.

After he signed over his land to the collectives, Uncle Marton returned home. Dropped off at the bus stop and not wanting to talk with anyone, he took a shortcut home via the garden path. Frankie was the first to see him coming down the path and we rushed to embrace him. We were so happy to see him! It was wonderful to have him home! I am sure he talked with my parents about his experiences in prison, but never in front of us. It was not that he did not trust us. Most of the parents felt it was best if political issues were not discussed in front of the children. It was safer that way for all concerned.

I was in fifth grade. We got used to the daily dose of propaganda from some of our teachers, we listened to what they said, and came to our own conclusions. Sadly enough, all of us had seen enough of the atrocities of the communist party in our little town. Only a small segment of our community embraced it. The rest complied simply to survive.

Most of the tradesmen in our town had to move into one building and form the shoemakers collective if they wanted to make shoes. The party also controlled the bakery, and they determined the type and size of bread to be baked. No more "specialty breads and fancy rolls," that was for the capitalists. This new type of plain bread everyone can afford. The two general stores were now under party management, and ordinary stock, once readily available, was no longer in stock.

The formation of the collective farms took more time. The communist party owned all land, but in the interim, the original owner of the land had to cultivate, sow, and harvest the crops. Some of the communist party members, accompanied by the AVH, went house to house to establish the amount of grain, potatoes and corn each household had to deliver to the collection site at the time of harvest. It did not matter if the crops were poor. Even if you did not have any left for your family, you must deliver your designated amount. If you owned a milk cow, which most people did, you had to deliver your assigned liter of milk to the collection site every day. Since our town was an agricultural community, most people had chickens. At the end of summer, the truck would come around and pick up the required number of chickens. A permit was issued for each household to butcher one pig per year. A portion of the meat and lard was taken to a collection site to feed the Russian army occupying our country. Trainload after trainload of foodstuff was daily shipped out of our country into Russia.

In order to establish the collective farms, they had to have farm equipment to work the fields. The families who had the most and best equipment were the "kulaks," the enemies of the state. Since most of them were in prison or deported, it was easy for the communists to come and confiscate their belongings. Therefore, it happened that one day they came and took all the farm equipment my parents owned and literally swept the attic of all the grain needed for the coming year. They took the potatoes from the cellar and left us with nothing. Nothing to eat and nothing to feed the cow, the two horses, and the few chickens they left. No matter how much he suffered, Father never embraced communism, he could not and would not compromise his principles and conviction. He said, "Don't hold onto material things, for your life is much more than the things you own. Possessions can be lost or taken away in a moment. Cultivate and pay attention to who you are on the inside, those qualities no one can take away from you. They can take everything away from me but they cannot take away my beliefs, my convictions, for without them, I am nothing. We are not responsible for other people's actions but we are accountable for our attitude and behavior. It is better if we are offended than if we offend others."

Father, facing the starvation of his family and his total inability to provide for his own, existing under a cruel and ruthless system, that was relentless in its purpose to wipe out every trace of human dignity, seeking to deprive men of their basic rights in an effort to gain control of the minds of men and turn them into a mindless machine that spouts the communist dogma, was coming to the end of his inner resources.

He was a gentle man, kind and generous, helping others. Always aware of the neighbor who needed help, both he and my Mother would share whatever we had, and so assisted families in need. For the neighbor who was sick and could not cultivate and plant his fields, Father would do it for him and harvest his crops so their family would not be in need. He never accepted money from anyone he helped. We rarely sat down at the dinner table alone as a family; he would always bring someone home who needed a meal. My parents were generous and loving.

I do not know just what happened to my Father on that day that was possibly the darkest day in his life. He could not provide for his family. Everything in our lives was controlled by this living terror, this evil despot, Stalin and his ruthless followers.

It was late at night, Frankie and I were asleep, when Mother, gently shaking my arm, whispered in my ear, "Saci, wake up. Please, go and talk to your Father, he'll listen to you. He is out in the back yard." Confused, I got out of bed and walked out into the darkness to find my Father. My mind was racing. What was wrong? It must be something terrible; otherwise, Mother would not have awakened me. No matter what happened, I could always depend on my parents, their love for us and their love for each other. Soon, I saw my Father sitting on log far away in the back yard, his head bowed low. Hesitantly, I drew near and sat down beside him. Why was I here? What was I supposed to say to this dear man, who was my beloved Father, who called me Saci from the day of my birth, meaning "little treasure?" I adored him. I nestled close to his side, not saying anything, just quiet beside him. What despair brought this strong man to this dark hour? Friends and neighbors sought his advice and encouragement. Now he was alone struggling with deepest anguish and hopelessness. I sensed more than I understood. My eyes slowly adjusted to the darkness while we both sat motionless, side-by-side. His form bending low, his hands resting on his knees, and then, I saw it. He had a black object in his hand. My mind flashed back to the time when I saw a similar object in the hands of the "bloody one." Cold fear gripped my soul. I trembled on the inside and could not control my shaking. Where did Father get this gun? Two years ago when our house had been ransacked the AVH did not find anything. We just sat there, a father and a daughter, not saying a word. I waited. Time passed very slowly in the darkness. Finally, at long last, his hand lightly touching my arm he simply said, "Time for you to go to bed." We stood up, his big hand holding my little one. We walked slowly across the long yard and into the house. Still holding my hand, with his other arm he embraced Mother. They put me to bed and I fell asleep, relieved.

Mother was an early riser. She was heading out to the well to draw fresh water when she came upon an amazing sight. There, on our front porch, stacked next to the front door, were several sacks of potatoes, onions, root vegetables, sacks of wheat for flour, corn to feed the few animals, and other foodstuff. Later, they found out that this gracious gift was from a family whom Father had helped years ago. Other neighbors and relatives shared and provided for our needs. That fall, just before the cold winter days two men in a truck arrived at our house with a load of coal. They were coal miners. Father had helped these men years ago before the war, and it was just at this time they decided to repay. Father was genuinely gracious, never expecting anything in return and always ready to help anyone in need. The principle of sowing and reaping is true indeed, for we reap what we sow.

Our parents always stressed the importance of education. Studying, and good grades, was a top priority. Most of our teachers closely followed the curriculum and never strayed into political dogma. A few of our teachers were hard-core communists and they seized every opportunity to indoctrinate us. We soon learned the difference. With the exception of a handful of students whose parents espoused communism and its ideology, the rest of us learned to go along and say what the teacher wanted to hear even though we did not believe it ourselves. The domestic purges continued. AVH's scope of action increased, assisted by a network of informants who provided covert surveillance on the dissenters. Most of us knew who the dissenters were, even though we never verbalized it. It was best to keep to our studies.

We received an excellent education. By the end of first grade, every student knew how to read. Without reading you cannot learn, was the motto of our teacher. Russian became a compulsory second language in 1951, along with Russian history and geography. Other subjects taught: literature, grammar, composition, history, geography, math, geometry, social studies, physics, chemistry, art, music, and gym. We remained in the same classroom. Our teachers moved from class to class. Every day we had homework that was due the next day. Every day we could be called upon to answer questions about our lessons. If selected, one stood, repeated the question, and gave an answer. Occasionally we solved math, geometry, or chemistry problems on the blackboard. No wonder we all studied hard. We did not want to be embarrassed in front of our classmates. Peer pressure worked in a positive way.

In spite of everything, we were still children and looked for fun where we could find it. We liked school and we liked living in a small town, we knew all our classmates and enjoyed all the extracurricular activities. School plays and concerts were always enjoyable and gave us an opportunity to perform for the entire community. Several times during the summer, my brother, our friends, and I would ride our bikes to Lake Balaton. It was a wonderful adventure. We enjoyed the beaches on the south shore of the lake and took a boat ride over to the north side to Tihany. There, we wandered through the beautiful yellow Abbey built in the 1400s. We explored all the out of-the-way places on the beach. In the late afternoon, we would take the boat back to the south side of the lake, pick up our bikes, and prepare for the three plus hours of riding back home. If we were lucky, we would catch a train, load up our bikes, and take the train to the closest stop near Kislang and we would be home in about an hour. Our parents, ever mindful of our childhood, tried to let us be children and have fun whenever they felt it would be safe. Our lives were uncertain; we never knew when the AVH would show up and disrupt our lives, or when the next wave of persecution would start, or who would be the next victim. However, our parents allowed us the freedom to enjoy our childhood only after all of our household chores were finished first.

One day the town crier had exciting news. We could hardly wait to hear it. Finally, after many years of waiting, electricity would be restored to every home. Sometime in 1952, radio speakers were delivered to each home. These speakers were connected to a central radio station with two channels, an AM and an FM station. On the AM station, communist propaganda blared all day long, but on the FM station, we could listen to classical music, operas, and popular Hungarian music. Electricity, what a marvel! Finally,

Mother could put away all the lamps and we could turn on the electric lights. Such brightness, growing up without it, we never knew what we were missing. We were thrilled to have lights in every room inside the house and also some outside. It was simple, run the wire from the pole to our house and connect the power. We even had streetlights illuminating our tiny town.

During part of this summer break, all schoolchildren were required to spend some time working on the collective farms. We were the new generation of communists and we must learn to obey and follow our glorious leaders and to give our allegiance to the party. On a set date, we gathered at our school and climbed aboard several military trucks, not knowing exactly where we were going. We only knew we were going to pick cotton at one of the collectives. We all looked at each other. What was cotton? All we knew was it grew in America and the slaves had to pick it. We studied in our history class the cruel way the poor slaves were treated. Hungary's climate is not suited for cotton growing. Yet, one of the goals of Rakosi, the faithful puppet of Russia and Stalin, was that we must be self-contained and produce everything our country needed. Many experimental crops were grown unsuccessfully and foolishly at great cost.

Russian soldiers drove the trucks and guarded us at gunpoint. Surely they were not afraid of less than one hundred children between the ages of ten and twelve? More likely they were wielding their power to intimidate us. Arriving at the fields, we picked up a burlap sack and were assigned rows. None of us had ever seen a cotton field before, so we did not know that the white cotton ball was within a sharp and pointy pod. We had to be very careful in removing the cotton ball or the sharp points would prick our fingers and cause them to bleed. Slowly, with forefinger and thumb, we gently pulled the cotton balls out of the plants and put them in the sacks. The soldiers noticed we were not making much progress so they started shouting, motioning with their guns for us to keep moving. We picked faster, our little fingers hurting, then after awhile, our backs hurt. We bent over picking, then tiring, crawled on the ground. Our bodies ached. We began talking among ourselves, remembering the poor slaves in America picking cotton for cruel taskmasters. We identified with those American slaves. Many of our countrymen were tortured, beaten, imprisoned or deported and we, at an early age, had to learn to submit without questioning, with mindless obedience to a corrupt system we did not believe in.

It was a very hot summer day. Filling our sack, we dragged it to the end of the row. A soldier would empty it on the truck, give it back, and we started picking again. At noon, we were given an hour lunch break. Another truck arrived with our food. Forming a line, we picked up a tin canteen, a tin cup and a spoon. We held out our canteen and a soldier poured a ladle full of soup in it and gave us a thick slice of communist issue bread. We would find all kinds of unusual things in the slice of bread, like bugs and such. We were also given a cup of water. Finding a place along the edge of the cotton fields, we sat on the ground with our friends and ate our measly lunch. After lunch, we picked up our sacks and resumed picking. We were tired, not being used to such work. Every time we slowed down the soldiers waved their guns and shouted, "Work faster, and keep moving."

When the electricity was restored in our town, we heard on the FM radio station the songs of Paul Robeson, an American son of a former slave. Known to Hungarians as the greatest bass-baritone singer of his time, he soon became a favorite. He championed the cause of the oppressed throughout his life. In the course of his many travels, he also visited the Soviet Union. We often listened to the songs of this talented man on the radio station and our favorite was "The Old Man River." He was the first Negro whose voice and life history I had come to know and admire, and, after all, he was acquainted with slavery.

Somewhere in the middle of the cotton field, above the shouts of the soldiers, rose the soft voice of a child singing the first lines of "Old Man River." Instantly the entire cotton field resounded with our voices singing and protesting our treatment as slaves. Feeling an extraordinary kinship to our slave counterparts across the ocean, we sang all afternoon and picked cotton. Singing those particular songs of the Negro slaves was our expression of protest. Yes, we were forced to work, but we did not submit willingly.

I cannot speak for all the children in that field, but as for me, I knew deep within, I may obey outwardly and even work against my will, but the real me, who I am and what I am, this communist system could never change. Communism would never be an ideology I would embrace; I suffered it first hand and experienced its cruelty against my family.

During the summer break, when we did not have to work in the collectives, occasionally I would accompany Father to the fields. He did not take me out there to work; he let me wander through the fields and meadows, picking wild flowers. Sitting in the grass, I listened to the sounds of summer and watched the tiny little lark soaring up in the sky; its beautiful song would fill the air. I would lie in the grass, gazing at the blue sky with fluffy white clouds, daydreaming. Dreams of being free, no wars, no terror-filled nights making me helpless and vulnerable, depriving me of people I loved. There in the fields, lying in the grass all alone, I was free. Father never probed or asked, he respected my secret thoughts. There in the fields among the wild flowers, my soul would find peace.

I hated the communists; they were cruel to my family. They had imprisoned Uncle Marton. They invaded my country and stole everything we owned and left us destitute. For what reason? Those days when I spent time with Father in the fields, I would pour out my heart to him, sharing how much I hated our neighbors who turned communist. Even though he suffered greatly at their hands, he would gently say, "Saci, hate only destroys you, not the object of your hatred." I heard him, but did not understand him. Deep in my heart, I wished all communists dead.

Father did not focus on the fear and terror of the communist activities around us, instead he deliberately drew our attention to activities that would create pleasant experiences for us. I loved being with him. He was patient, listened, and always took the opportunity to teach me about the world. After visiting relatives and walking homewards in the night, he would take my hand and we would gaze at the starlit sky, as he pointed out the constellations. We would watch the shooting stars on summer nights. During the long winter evenings, we would read books, play cards, and table games he would create for us. He so wanted to give us a normal and carefree childhood. Whenever it was possible, we would visit relatives enriching us with new experiences.

Aunt Irene and Uncle John and their son Johnnie lived in Budapest. They would spend several weeks during the summer break with us. Johnnie was a sickly child and the fresh air in the country improved his health. We were delighted when they visited. We explored the countryside and took Johnnie on bike rides. Soccer was our favorite summer game. Johnnie loved feeding the animals and playing with our dog and cats.

Aunt Irene was a talented and creative seamstress. She sewed for most of the wives of the Hungarian National Soccer Team. Women from all over Budapest wanted her to design their clothes. She worked hard sewing all day and many times way into the night to finish some of her beautiful creations for a special event. During her visit, she would make dresses for mother and me.

Uncle John drove a BMW motorbike with a sidecar. When we heard his bike stop in front of our house, we knew we were in for a treat. At the end of their visit, we would return with them for four to six weeks of vacation in Budapest. As much as Johnnie loved to be in the country, we were looking forward as much to visiting the city. All of us would pile on the motorbike and in the sidecar and we had the thrill of our lives as Uncle John was driving. He never drove the same route but always surprised us. Our favorite route was along the banks of the Danube.

Budapest is the capital of Hungary. It is a city split in two by the Danube River, with many bridges and islands. On the right bank of the Danube is Pest and on the left bank, up on the hillside, is Buda. Buda offers a more picturesque sight, with historical buildings, castles, forts, palaces, monasteries and churches. It will always remain the royal city with its historical monuments. Pest is more contemporary, with operas, theatres, sport stadiums, museums, amusement park and the zoo. The lovely City Park and the magnificent Parliament building are located on this side also. While spending summers with Aunt Irene, I had the wonderful privilege of exploring the city, visiting the amusement park and the zoo, and exploring Margit Island. We would take the streetcar into the heart of the city, then walk through the historical streets of Buda, and spend all day discovering the treasures. We would stroll along the shores of the Danube and wander through Pest. I could never see enough or spend a long enough time there, but the promise of returning next summer eased the disappointment when it was time to go home.

Despite considerable sacrifice on their part, our parents gave us the opportunity to visit relatives in different towns and villages and to take field trips with classmates. They nurtured my desire and curiosity to always want to see around the corner; my irresistible call to adventure, to discover and explore new places and meet new people.

GRADUATION

In 1954, we entered the classroom knowing this would be our last year together as a class. At the end of this school year, we would be graduating and facing the unknown future, the future that was veiled from our eyes. As most thirteen and fourteen-year-old children we had little idea which career to choose, no problem, we were living under a system that made our decisions for us. It was a year of bittersweet memories. As a class we shared many experiences. We survived the war and its aftermath. We endured the communist purging and tasted the life of "owning all things in common" and working on collective farms. Early in life we learned the responsibility of taking care of ourselves.

Outwardly, no one expressed an opinion about the communist dictatorship, because we could not trust anyone. We had no freedom of speech, no freedom of any kind. Yet questions churned in my mind. Deep down, I knew that we were not meant to live like this. If I was held responsible for the choices I made, should I not be given the freedom to choose to learn about other cultures?

Should I not be able to read the works of authors who were considered "enemies of the state?" Why were we limited in learning about only half of our world? Why were they misrepresenting the facts and portraying the people in Western Europe and the United States as "warmongers" and "capitalists" who exploit people? They would not trust us to learn and draw our own conclusions; they had to force their propaganda, by whatever means they deemed necessary, until we completely and mindlessly conformed without question. Yes, I learned and repeated the right answers they wanted to hear, but I wanted a true education. My parents desperately wanted me to have a better life than one working on the collective farms. We studied hard but our future was very uncertain; our future was in the hands of a few communist party leaders in our town. Higher education was not determined by how well you scored on your aptitude test, but by how loyal you were to the party.

After returning from spring break, our homeroom teacher handed us a blank sheet of paper and asked us what we wanted to be, which career we wanted to pursue. At fourteen, I already knew what I wanted to be, but I could not write it on that paper. I wanted to be free! Instead, I wrote a teacher, since I loved history and geography. I also thought I would like to design and sew clothes like Aunt Irene. If I had the freedom to write what was deep in my heart, I would have written that I wanted to travel, to see the exciting and forbidden places of the world. Hungarians were not allowed to leave the country, except to travel to the Soviet Union, and who wanted to see the place where most of our fellow citizens had been deported?

The end of school year was fast approaching. We were cramming for the final exams, a written exam for all of our subjects. We could not sit in our usual seats; we were assigned to every other seat. Only a blank piece of paper and a pen were permitted on our desktop. We walked single file to the teacher's desk pulled the test questions from the basket in front of our teacher, returned to our seat and read our question. We had one hour to write our answer. After handing in our paper, we were excused to leave the room. The following day we had our oral exam, also for all of our subjects. Upon entering the classroom, I discovered that the school principal, our homeroom teacher, and the teacher who taught that particular subject were all sitting at the large desk. No other classmates were present in the room. I stood in front of the desk and waited for my instructions. The teacher read the question and I had a few minutes to think and formulate my answer. The principal and homeroom teacher had the privilege to ask any question regarding that particular subject. The rest of the class was in the hall awaiting their turn. The oral exams were completed in two days.

The waiting was agonizing. All three teachers graded us on the oral exam and the written exam. Meanwhile, we compared notes and talked about our own experience. We received different questions and hoped that we gave the correct answers. Next, we were given our report cards, then, at last, we could plan for our graduation ceremony. The final news we were all waiting to hear was who among us was selected to pursue higher education.

When the teacher read my name I was shocked and amazed. I was accepted into the liberal arts program at Teleki Blanka, an all girl's school in Szekesfehervar.

GOING AWAY TO SCHOOL

Summer vacation was busy, as we planned and prepared for school in September. I would live in a dorm. We received a list of articles I would need, along with a description of the uniform I would wear. The color was navy blue, with buttons down the back, long sleeves, with detachable sleeves for warmer days, and white detachable collar and cuffs. The length of the uniform was just below the knee. Aunt Irene was coming to spend some time with us during the summer and I knew she would sew my uniform.

It was a summer of many emotions. Annie was not going to school, she was moving to live with her aunt in Sopron, an old historical city dating back to the Romans. Sopron lies on the Austrian-Hungarian border, a city rich in beautiful architecture spanning several centuries. Annie was only gone for a few days and I already missed her. Helen and Judith were spending the summer vacation visiting relatives. My moods changed from reflective to thoughtful, to lighthearted. I was entering a new phase of my life. Already friends and schoolmates were going on their separate ways; soon I would be leaving also. I was the only one from Kislang who was going to Szekesfehervar, to live in the dorm. I would meet new girls and make new friends. Under different circumstances, it would have been exciting. Now, I was saying good-bye to old friends, family, and everything familiar.

It was a difficult time for my Mother and Father also. I was almost six years old when Father came home, and eight years later, we would be saying good-bye. During those years, he poured his heart into my life, preparing me for this time. The values and principles that guided his life became the foundation of my life. He had been tempered by the experiences of his life; on the other hand, I was high-spirited and strong willed with a large dose of stubbornness. As a small child I learned the value of proper behavior, since I did not want to bring shame upon my parents. Deep in the recesses of my heart, however dimly lit, I remembered God; the God of my early childhood. Above all, I was afraid of displeasing Him. Even though I seldom said my memorized prayers and church attendance was forbidden, I knew that someday I would have to meet God and give an account of my life. The old question haunted me, would there be enough good deeds to outweigh the bad?

Why is it that life changing events are always hard? We had been preparing, especially Mother, so I would have the necessary clothing, bedding, towels, toiletries and everything that was required to live in the dorm. It was hard to say good-bye to Uncle Marton. He was hugging me, kissing me, and admonishing me to take care of myself. How often Frankie, my little brother, and I teased each other, yet we were best friends. I already missed him. This was the first time that I was going away alone, not visiting relatives, but facing the unknown. I had no other choice. The collectives were not for me.

I had visited Szekesfehervar many times before. A former Roman settlement, it is one of the oldest towns in Hungary. Zigzagging through the narrow streets in the historical section of the town, we arrived at the dorm. It was an impressive old building, a former cloister, closed during the communist purging. Huge, solid wooden doors opened as we rang the doorbell. An attendant ushered us into the courtyard for registration. A guide accompanied us to the bedroom and pointed out my pre-assigned bed, making sure that we had brought everything exactly as directed. Mother made up the bed while I unpacked my clothes into the locker assigned to me. The nightstand beside the bed held the toiletries. Everything had a place, and everything had to be in its place. After Mother and Father helped me settle in, they were instructed to leave. No long good-byes and lingering visits were permitted. Walking with them to the door, the guard opened it, and closed it as soon as they were outside, blocking them from my view. Slowly I walked back to my bedroom. Only then, did I really look at my new surroundings. I now lived in a long rectangular room with bunk beds lining both sides of the wall with only a nightstand between the beds, and lockers lining one wall of the room. Twenty-four girls shared this room. By the end of the afternoon, the entire dormitory was full as everyone arrived. All the freshmen had a guided tour of the building, which was to be our home for the next four years.

The two storied, U-shaped building had served as a cloister and a private school for over a hundred years. Each wing housed two floors of dorm rooms with twenty- four to thirty students on each floor. Also living on the premises was the school principal and her family, the dean and her husband, both professors, and the building caretaker. We ate our meals in a huge dining room and shared a large military style washroom with sinks, washtubs and showers. Of the four hundred students who attended the school, approximately one hundred and twenty lived in the dorm.

The dean and the principal welcomed the freshmen and the returning upper classmen, explaining the rules, regulations, requirements while living in the dormitory. Loud talking, yelling, screaming and running through the hallways was forbidden. Every hour of our day was scheduled and the rules were strictly enforced.

Every morning, at five o'clock, the dean would march up and down the hallways ringing a big cowbell, announcing it was time to get up. There was no second call. We jumped out of bed and hurried in the washroom to clean up and get dressed for the day. Our uniform and shoes must be spotlessly clean. Before breakfast, we made our bed and tidied the small area around our bed. Everything had a place, and everything had to be in its place. At six o'clock, the bell would call us for breakfast. We sat at long tables with benches and were served family style. Proper and perfect table manners were expected. I felt sorry for the girls who did not learn proper table manners at home, most of the time they were openly ridiculed. While we were enjoying our breakfast, the dean made her rounds inspecting the dorm rooms. Before she dismissed us she would announce the names of those whose beds were not neat or had left articles out of place. After breakfast, we had time for last minute preparations, then we reported to the study hall, picked up our books, and at 7:30 a.m. lined up at the front gate, four abreast, to walk to our school. All the schools had caps that identified the type of the school and those attending there. Our colors were navy and we always wore the caps on the city streets. On our way to school, we would cross paths with the students from the other schools in town. We maintained proper decorum at all times, no waving, or calling out, or breaking the ranks.

School started at 8:00 a.m. and the last bell rang at 1:00 p.m. Monday through Saturday. . The school building was over one hundred years old, but very well maintained. I guess when you live in an old historical town it is not unusual that the buildings are old. We received our classroom assignment upon registration so we each headed for our homeroom. We stayed in our classroom except for chemistry lab and gym. Education was important. Our teachers demanded that we learn and maintain a certain grade point average or we would not remain there.

When the last bell announced the end of the school day, those of us living in the dormitory lined up in front of the school building, in the same formation, and walked back to our new home. Putting our books away, we prepared for lunch. The ringing of the bell called us to line up in the hall single file and quietly enter the dining room. Following lunch, we had a study hall period to do our homework. The afternoon study hall ended at 5:00 p.m. allowing for a half an hour break before dinner. At 7:00 p.m., we had another hour of study hall and at 8:00 p.m., we had our assembly where the dean and principal would review the activities of the day. Our teachers would have reported our progress in the classroom including the grades we received. The dean would read those reports aloud to the entire assembly. At

9:00 p.m., it was time for bed. The dean made her rounds, checking that we were all in bed and then she turned the lights out, announcing the end of our day. Each day our routine was the same. On Sunday, after lunch, we were given a two hour leave but we must stay in town. This privilege was granted only if we had good grades. We signed out at the gate and signed in upon returning.

We could go home during winter and spring breaks. Our parents were not encouraged to visit. The curriculum was demanding. It was very clear, we were here to study. We had no time for entertainment. We were encouraged to participate in sports, but only if we maintained at least a B grade point average. We could not choose our coursework, the curriculum was set for the four years, and we needed to complete all the studies assigned for each year. The first year curriculum included: Hungarian grammar, literature, social studies, history, algebra, geometry, physics, chemistry, biology, Russian, German, music, and gym. The second year, French was added to my language studies.

Our lives were structured and regimented to the minutest of detail. I felt like Pavlov's dog, all day long responding to the ringing of the bell. We did not have to think when to do what, all the thinking was done for us. Our only focus was to study to prepare for the future. The future, what did the future hold for us?

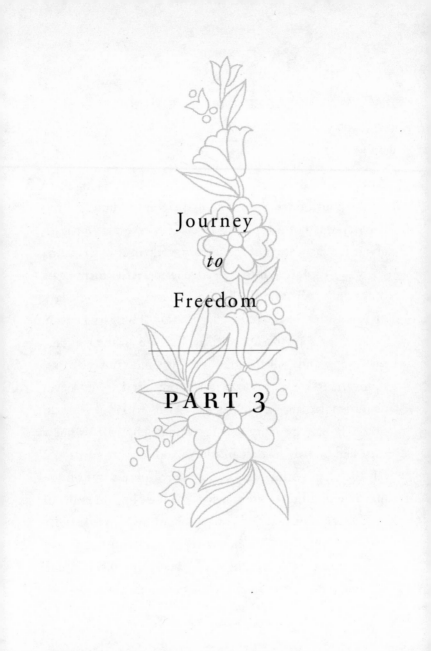

Journey *to* Freedom

PART 3

TASTE OF FREEDOM

After the death of Stalin in 1953 changes were taking place on the political scene. In school, the political unrest in our country was not a topic for discussion. We did not learn about the discontent of the factory workers or of the farmers who were forced into collective farms. After many years of war, of occupation by the communists, of a chronic lack of necessities, of unending deprivation, Hungarians were looking for some basic comforts. Despite all the communist propaganda, all the grandiose five and ten year plans, Hungarians knew this was not Utopia, and would never be. Frustrated and helpless in the face of AVH (Hungarian Secret Police) brutality and repression, Hungarians knew they had already lost all freedoms and human rights and felt they had nothing left to lose. Civil unrest was on the march. Conditions were ripe for rebellion. In September of 1956, I started my second year of school, and I was familiar with the routine. Khrushchev replaced Stalin but it had little impact on the Hungarian leadership and daily life remained the same. In the classroom and dormitory, we were isolated from much of the news and events happening in our country. Those classmates who commuted to school linked us to the outside world.

On October 23, 1956, we were in school when we heard about a spontaneous demonstration, including many students, marching to the Parliament demanding reforms. While unable to ignore the demonstration, Parliament had no intention of granting reforms and ordered repression by force. Two days later the entire country broke into a revolution. Petofi Sandor was a Hungarian poet beloved by many. His words inspired the cause of the revolution in 1848, and resounded again in 1956. In his poem, he calls to the Hungarians to "Rise for our country calls us. In this hour, decide what ever befalls us. Shall we become free or remain slaves?" (I can only translate the meaning of his stirring poem). These words reflected the deepest meaning and cause of the revolution, our ancient love of liberty. However, his words did not explain how this small nation found the courage, the bravery, to challenge the mighty Soviet Union.

The unarmed demonstrators marched on to Radio Budapest, echoing the cry of the people, "freedom of speech, freedom of worship, we shall never be slaves." The AVH opened fire, and the revolution began in earnest. By nightfall, Budapest's great Stalin statue was pulled from its foundation. All symbols of Communist rule were violently torn down and destroyed. The red stars, the symbol of communism, were cut from the center of every Hungarian flag.

Political prisoners, among them Cardinal Mindszenty, were freed. Even without television, the news of the freedom fight spread like wildfire. When we heard the news, not one student remained in the building. Our teachers could not hold us back. We were out on the street joining the demonstrators, marching to the Headquarters of the Russian Military. All along the way, people were tearing down the symbols of communism.

In front of the headquarters we chanted, "Russians go home." We demanded, "Freedom of speech, freedom of religion, freedom from slavery," with many waving the "new" Hungarian flag with the red star missing from the center. We sang the Hungarian national anthem, which begins with the words, "God bless the Magyar (Hungarian)..." God, whose name we were forbidden to mention for years.

The Russian general pleaded with us to "Go home, after all, we are your friends, your brothers and we do not want to hurt you. Go home peacefully." Then he retreated inside. The demonstration continued, marching through the streets of the town, singing, chanting, demanding freedom. It was late at night when we returned to our dorm.

On October 24, 1956, ten thousand Russian troops with tanks entered Budapest. They opened fire on the demonstrators before the Parliament. By the end of the day, fighting had spread all over the city and the country. In Szekesfehervar, we were also demonstrating in front of the Russian Military Headquarters when the Russian tanks rolled in through the side streets. They opened fire on the unarmed demonstrators, killing eight students between the ages of eighteen and twenty. The tanks continued to roll. We were forced to run for cover. Reluctantly we returned to our dorm. With the huge gates safely locked, we turned off the lights and gathered upstairs in the assembly room, listening to the sounds of gunfire, and watching as Russian tanks positioned themselves in front of our building. We all heard and understood their orders spoken in Russian. We were warned, they would blow up our building at any sign of opposition.

Imre Nagy became the newly elected Premier of Hungary. He negotiated with Moscow to withdraw their troops. The Russians refused unless the freedom fighters laid down their arms. Of course, the freedom fighters refused to lay down their arms until the Russians left. During the night of October 29, the Russian forces pulled out of Budapest leaving their dead behind them. However, the main Russian tank force along the Danube was still in place. October 30, 1956, major Russian units started to leave Budapest. The freedom fighters found themselves in command of the city. Russian units continued to withdraw. The entire nation celebrated the victory. Church bells rang across the city.

During the fighting, it was difficult to find out what was happening. In the morning hours, hundreds of residents from all over Budapest were inspecting the damage. Streets were choked with rubble, fifteen-block area in the southeast part of Budapest showed the ravages of a full-scale war. The Russian dead, in scores, lay beside burned out tanks, armored cars, and guns. People wandered the streets in disbelief that they had driven the enemy out. Several free radio stations reported that Russian reinforcements were coming from Romania and the Ukraine. The Hungarian army posted tanks to defend the country. More Russians were arriving from the eastern border.

Imre Nagy proclaimed Hungarian neutrality and appealed to the United Nations for protection. Our pleas were ignored around the western world. We waited and hoped, but no news came. Not a word, nor an offer of help from anywhere. The world was silent.

November 4, 1956. Our freedom was short lived. Russian tanks thundered into Budapest and other major cities throughout the country, crushing the revolution. Russian MIG fighters flew over Budapest. The cost in human lives was estimated around three thousand.

November 6, 1956, the radio station held by the freedom fighters sent a farewell message: "People of the world, in the name of liberty we are asking you to help. Listen to our cry. Extend to us brotherly hands. People of the world save us. Help! Help! Help!" After this entreaty, there was only silence from the free world.

Reinforcements of Russian infantry arrived. Tanks and artillery were killing thousands indiscriminately, and the infantry marched house to house killing the freedom fighters systematically. Russian troops searched and deported thousands of Hungarians to slave labor camps in Russia. Imre Nagy was captured and later executed. Sporadic outbursts of fighting continued in Budapest and in the provinces. Russians looted the city and threatened to starve out any freedom fighters left alive. A general strike gripped the country. The Russians continued a nationwide roundup of freedom fighters implicated in the revolution. Janos Kadar seized the government. He asked the nation to "welcome the soldiers of the Russian army who have helped us overcome the counterrevolution."

This Russian help included the public hanging, from the Danube bridges in Budapest, many freedom fighters. The Russians tightened their dragnet for everyone who in any way had been engaged in the fight for freedom. Hungarians by the thousands were escaping into Austria and Yugoslavia. Approximately 200,000 Hungarians fled the country. The rest of the Hungarians silently awaited their fate.

Our fight for freedom was unplanned, unaided. The freedom fighters had no outside help, only each other. This freedom fight is a story of glory, of the love of liberty, and a memorial to the brave of Hungary. It is also a cry that fighters for freedom, wherever they are, should not stand and die alone.

The most unexpected and amazing segment of the freedom forces was the youth: boys and girls in their teens and early twenties. During our formative years, we were subjected to communist indoctrination and discipline. We heard traditional values ridiculed and reviled by our instructors. Nevertheless, in the battle, the youth turned the tide, proving that Hungarian national pride and love of freedom had survived a decade of Communism, and Communist indoctrination.

Sweet were the victories, bitter the defeat. Freedom was so close, yet so far away. Will it forever remain only a dream? We were not alone, millions of people through-out the ages have paid the ultimate sacrifice to be free and sadly, like us, were not always successful.

Our school closed indefinitely. We returned home to await our future. One of our neighbors had a short wave radio and we lived for the news reports telling us how many of our compatriots escaped to the west. Annie's mother had good news to share. Sometime in the early part of November, Annie crossed over into Austria and from there she traveled to Switzerland. Helen's brother and several of his friends also made it to Austria and from there immi-grated to the United States.

Along with the success stories, there were far more stories of those who tried but did not make it. Under the circumstances, death was preferable to being captured. The rounding up of anyone implicated in the freedom fight continued, as did the general strike. Fear, tension, and uncertainty shrouded like a fog over the country. The New Year did not promise a bright future. Schools remained closed. Public assemblies, group meetings and gatherings were against the law.

The heavily guarded Austrian border made escape through there next to impossible, so thousands of refugees escaped into Yugoslavia, but as months passed that border was also tightly patrolled. Our most reliable information came via shortwave radio's daily broadcast reporting the number of people crossing the borders. By January of 1957, only a small number of people crossed over into Yugoslavia successfully. I listened to the news and was delighted to hear about the success stories, but for me, it seemed an impossible dream. We did not live near the border, I had no idea how to go about escaping, and by 1957, it was useless even to think about it.

On Friday, February 1, 1957, I stopped in at the general store to purchase a few things. Several shoppers were waiting in line at the cash register. Turning to leave, I noticed our family friend Elizabeth standing beside a man I did not recognize. I walked over to greet her. She turned to the man beside her and asked him, "Don't you recognize her?" He stared at me for a long time, trying to remember. Elizabeth asked me "Do you remember him?" I shook my head, "No." As he gazed at me, recognition slowly dawned, and a gentle smile spread across his eyes and face as he said, "Saci, you have grown up." Alex? It cannot be. The piercing blue eyes were so familiar, but could it really be Alex? Whatever happened to his beautiful, blond curly hair? He was pale, his shoulders stooped. No, it could not be him. Hesitantly I asked, "Alex?" He nodded and clasped my hand. It had been years since I last saw him.

My mind was racing to remember what I knew of him and his whereabouts. His life was a mystery; very few people in Kislang knew what he did. In his early twenties, he was involved in politics. It was common knowledge that he vehemently opposed communism. Rumors had it that he became an agent and helped people escape from the country. He was part of a network of men and women who risked their own lives to help others escape. In the early 1950s, he was captured and imprisoned in the notorious prison at 60 Andrassy Boulevard in Budapest. The prison was known as the house of terror, and speaking its very name filled one with dread. Originally, it was built as a private residence. In 1945, the house became the headquarters of the secret police. Soon the whole block was annexed and the walls between houses were demolished. A prison was created in the labyrinth of cellars. The AVH owned the building until 1956. It was a prison of torture and terror. Those who were fortunate to be released were a shadow of their former selves. Most never left. Alex and all those imprisoned there were set free by the freedom fighters in October of 1956.

Elizabeth invited me for dinner and to meet Rose, Alex's wife. After dinner Elizabeth, Rose and I were sitting around the table enjoying a cup of tea catching up on family events and my experiences in school, while Alex and his father were quietly talking at the other side of the room. I was more interested in the bits and pieces of conversation I overheard between Alex and his father. Alex had just returned from meeting with someone in Budapest. He was sharing news that obviously distressed him very much. Someone had proposed to him to join the new Kadar regime, or to make plans to leave the country immediately. Two pairs of eyes locked together, both sorrowful, looking at his father he said, "You know my decision; I'll be making plans to leave soon."

"Take me with you," impulsively the words popped out. Startled, all eyes turned to me. A long silence followed my outburst. I could hear the ticking of the clock on the table. I was waiting and could not take my eyes from Alex's face, waiting for his answer. Frozen in place, I could not believe what I had asked of him. What in the world got into me?

Finally, Alex spoke with grim patience, "You don't know what you are asking of me." He was right, I did not know. His life was in danger. He was a wanted man. He did not need the added burden of worrying about a fifteen-year-old girl. "Take me with you" the words came involuntarily. Dismayed by my request, he turned to his father and asked, "What should I do?" Slowly and deliberately his father responded, "She will be fine, son, she is her father's daughter."

Alex stared at me, with those piercing blue eyes, very grave, "You have to follow my orders, no questions asked. You will have to trust me. Our lives depend on your complete obedience. Can you do that?"

"Yes, I can." I answered with a firm resolution. "I will get a message to you when you need to know," his voice was expressionless.

On my way home that evening I could not believe this turn of events. I never once realized the enormity of my decision. I understood the danger, yet I was not afraid. I had a strange feeling, hard to describe, as if someone else was making this decision for me.

On Sunday afternoon, February 3, 1957, I decided to go downtown with friends to see the movies. We were standing around talking, when Rose's brother stopped to say hello. That seemed unusual. I knew his family lived in town, but I could not remember ever talking with him. We exchanged polite pleasantries. As he prepared to leave to join his friends, he said, "Tuesday morning at 6:00 am, be at the bus station. No packages, bags, only a small purse." He looked straight into my eyes, making sure I understood the message. With a small nod of acknowledgement, I whispered, "I am looking forward to seeing your sister."

For two days, I was tormented by feelings of secrecy. How was I going to tell my parents that I was leaving, and, furthermore, that I had made this decision myself? I had left little Kislang for higher education over a year ago. I had been raised in a regimented, institutional lifestyle. For years the government had decided for us, dictated every aspect of our lives. I loved my family very much. Would I ever see them again? The call of freedom was beckoning. The tug at my heart was so strong, a most unusual feeling, like it was meant to be. This was to be my destiny.

ESCAPE

On Tuesday morning, February 5, 1957, I rose early, dressed, hugged, and kissed my parents, my brother, and Uncle Marton and walked to the bus station. I could not say "Good-Bye"; that was too final as if I would never see them again. Before dawn, the streets were deserted. I looked at all the familiar sights, etching each forever in my mind, I would not ever wanting to forget this place. This was my farewell. In the darkness, all alone, I was saying good-bye to everything I loved. I was walking toward an unknown future on a perilous road filled with danger. What will happen if we fail? I would not allow myself to think about that.

Several passengers were already waiting in line, sighing with relief I did not recognize anyone. I waited at the edge of the crowd. More people were arriving, among them Alex and Rose. I remained in place, they saw me, made eye contact, but remained aloof. At 6:00 a.m., the bus pulled in and we started boarding. I waited in the back, allowing others to go before me. Alex and Rose stepped in front of me. They purchased tickets to Polgardi, a small town with a railroad station. I had a season pass. The driver punched my ticket. He recognized me and commented that I always took the later bus with all the students. Where was I going so early in the morning? Of all the mornings, he had to be chatty today. I mumbled something about meeting a girl-friend in Polgardi. More passengers were waiting to board. Glad to end the conversation, I moved on to find a seat.

The bus stopped at Polgardi and several people got off. I said good-bye to the driver, reminding him that I would see him in the evening on his return run. I knew the town. Allowing Alex to take the lead, I followed them at a distance. It was obvious that we had to pretend that we did not know each other. One more hurdle; I knew several students from Polgardi. I was hoping I would not meet any of them this morning. Alex walked to the ticket office and purchased tickets to Veszprem. This was going to be easy. I also purchased a ticket to Veszprem. For over two hours, we had not said a word to each other and I wondered for just how much longer. Soon he would have to say some-thing. I could not read his mind. Remembered my promise of obedience and no questions, I chose a seat at a distance, but always keeping them in clear view.

I followed them as we boarded the train to Veszprem. I was looking for a seat, when he gently pushed my arm to a seat across from them. The train was pulling out. Waiting, I looked out the window, prepared to play this game of pretense. I surreptitiously glanced around our coach, relieved that I did not recognize any of the passengers. Rose and I continued looking out the window. Occasionally I would glance at her and notice a slight twinkle of amusement in her eyes.

The conductor came and asked for our tickets. Pulling out my ticket, I handed it to him. Just then, I remembered we were not allowed to travel anywhere without legal permission from the local police and then we had to register with the police at our destination. What would I say if he asks for my identification card? Trying not to look anxious I watched him while he cancelled my ticket, I politely said "thank you" when he handed it back. He acknowledged it with a slight nod of his head and moved on to the other passengers. Our eyes met. Alex was evaluating me. There was a hint of approval in them. I knew I placed them in a difficult situation and I was determined to do my best to hold up my end of the bargain.

We arrived in Veszprem. Why here I wondered? I soon discovered his reason. He needed to see someone in the small village of Zsofia Puszta, which was located a short distance from Veszprem. After an hour or so of walking through town and the adjacent countryside, we found the address. His friend John lived here with his elderly parents. Even in their simple greeting, the friendship and camaraderie between the two men was evident. As fellow prisoners, Alex could not leave without letting his friend know they both were in danger. I watched the faces of the elderly couple. They loved their son, and they had the privilege of having him home for only a short time. With tears, his mother talked about the future and the joy of having him home as she bustled about the kitchen preparing refreshments. I shared her pain and heartbreak. Recognizing the danger to her son, she found the address of a relative in Canada. John could go there and start a new life. She split the seam in the belt of John's winter coat and sewed the address inside. Everyone knew there was no choice, he would have to leave.

Piercing pain was choking me. I ached for them. It was agony to watch the three of them say good-bye. The parents were old. They realized, even if their son did make it to Canada, they would never see him again. John knew it also. How could he leave them in their old age? Who would look after them? They walked us to the gate, stood there, holding onto each other, and waved until we were out of sight.

Zsofia Puszta had no public transportation, so we walked through several small villages and towns toward

Herend and Ajka. In small towns and villages, everyone knows everyone. Strangers in town automatically attract curiosity. The AVH, the communist sympathizers, and the Russian soldiers were busy rounding up all those participating in the freedom fight. We were not safe walking the street. Alex was setting the pace we needed to reach Ajka before dark. John was sure we could catch a bus there. I had no problem keeping up since I was used to walking everywhere. The urgency of getting out was driving Alex relentlessly.

Arriving in Ajka, we boarded the last bus that evening taking workers home to outlying towns and villages. After a long day, they were tired and eager to get home. Several of the passengers were suspicious of our presence on the bus and curious as to just who we were. Very late in the evening, we arrived in Ukk. Alex planned to catch a train heading southwest toward the tri-country border of Hungary, Austria, and Yugoslavia. It was so late, the streets were deserted, with hardly a light filtering through some of the windows. The villagers were sleeping. Small towns and villages are similar all over Hungary with fenced in yards and gates locked, especially at night. The handful of workers getting off the bus disappeared into the night, eager to get home. We were quickly walking through the town to the railroad station located at the far edge of town, when loud, boisterous voices broke the silence of the night speaking in a language all too familiar to any Hungarian. Russian soldiers were walking up the street toward us. It would be disastrous for us to meet them. No one said a word. We all knew we were in grave danger and had to act quickly. Already walking single file and close to the fences, what were we to do? We had halted by a house with a picket fence with several loose and missing boards. Without a word, the four of us crawled through to the other side and there found a deserted house, most of it lay in rubble. We could hear the heavy footsteps of the soldiers getting closer, but the darkness gave us all the protection we needed and we just had to hurry behind those walls for cover. In a matter of minutes, they were passing by the house. Silent and cold, we huddled there in the ruined house until 4:00 a.m.

At dawn, we must find the railroad station. Alex needed us to catch the commuter train where we would be able to mingle with the workers and get lost in the crowd. At the end of the road, there it stood, all lit up. We were approaching the station from the rear of the building, with the waiting room and ticket office at the front. Walking along the side of the building, we turned the corner and walked into four Russian soldiers. Without any hesitation, we greeted them and stepped into the waiting room. Wow! That was close! We purchased our tickets and waited for the train. The countryside was swarming with Russian soldiers. Would they return to the station? We dare not look suspicious. "Act normal, do not draw attention to yourself," I reminded myself.

The whistle of the approaching train broke into my reverie. It was time to board. When we used public transportation, we did not sit together since we did not want to arouse suspicion. We all boarded the same coach and found seats within view of each other. I chose a seat next to the window. Sitting there, I could not help but consider what this day would hold for us. Alex did not share sufficient information to satisfy my curiosity. I just followed his orders and did as I was told. The train was pulling out of the station and I found myself staring out into the early morning darkness avoiding conversation with other passengers around me.

The train stopped several times, picking up more passengers going to work. The daily riders carried on a lively conversation with each other. A man walked into our coach to inform his friends with the news that the train was loaded with Russian soldiers inspecting everyone. My heart skipped a beat. I was so far from home and my identification card registered me as a student in Szekesfehervar. Their first question would be, if they even bothered to ask, "Just what are you doing here, when travel is against orders, and you do not even possess a valid proof indicating that you may travel?" I searched for Alex, he and Rose were standing up, soon John followed. I knew it was my turn to follow his lead. We were walking toward the connecting platform when Alex calmly whispered, "We have to jump the train." What! Jump the train. Did he really say that? My mind was racing having never jumped a train before. I had seen a movie once where the main character jumped a train and broke his legs. His voice brought me back to reality. "John, you go first. Be sure you clear the telephone poles. Rose, you're next. Saci, pay attention! Jump when I tell you, roll on the ground, and lie still." Numbly, I walked to the bottom of the steps and waited for my order. "Jump!" I did, and rolled several feet down the gravel along the side of the tracks and remained there to stunned to move. I heard Alex jump. We lay at the side of the tracks waiting for the train to pass before I tried to move. I was taking inventory. I did not feel any pain, my legs were moving, my arms felt fine. Slowly I stood up and joined the group. Incredibly we were not hurt.

Alex led us across the railroad tracks toward the woods and he talked as he walked. For the first time, he was sharing the details of his plan with us, "We are not too far from Zalaegerszeg. Since it is no longer safe for us to use public transportation, we will have to continue on foot. This western part of Hungary is hilly and forested providing us with cover, but we will not be walking through towns or villages, and we will have to avoid public roads to be safe." Pulling a small compass from his pocket, he checked his direction. He and John led the way, with Rose and I following. He became more talkative since we were all alone. He walked with confidence, as if he knew where he was. After while he said, "In a short time we will see a draw well in a clearing and we can drink the water since it is good." Sure enough, we came upon the draw well. Satisfying our thirst, we continued.

It was Thursday morning February 7, 1957, with patches of snow on the ground, as my journey to freedom continued on foot. I was a good sport and never admitted to being tired as we trudged though ravines and the heavy undergrowth of shrubs and bushes. It was a treat when we walked upon an easy stretch of woods with only grass and moss on the ground. We had nothing to eat or drink. Alex kept telling us to eat snow. Well, if I ate snow, it would turn into liquid. Eventually the liquid had to go somewhere, and there was nowhere to "go" out in the woods! I was very careful to eat only a very small amount of snow.

Alex was so at home in these woods. He knew exactly where he was. After the sun set, he led us to a small village and to a specific house. He reached over the top of the fence, unlatched the gate, and we walked into the yard. He knocked and a man in his late fifties opened the door. Surprise and delight shown on his face when he recognized Alex. The two men embraced and slapped each other on the back. Opening his front door wide he urged us to come in. His wife and elderly parents were sitting around the kitchen table eating supper. Alex introduced us to the family and shared with them our intentions to escape. Our host set out extra plates and invited us to join them for supper. It felt so good to remove the heavy winter coat and sweater, to sit down, and enjoy the hot bowl of soup. With her kind brown eyes the grandmother kept watching me and shortly after dinner led me to the bedroom and insisted that I go to bed. It was so nice to snuggle down in the featherbed with big feather pillows and duvet so reminiscent of Grandmother's bed, but tonight was not a night for memories. My body was aching and tired, and my head barely hit the pillow before I was sound asleep.

Everyone was up enjoying a cup of coffee when Rose came and woke me up. It seemed I had just fallen asleep and now it was morning already. I dressed quickly and joined them for breakfast.

Friday, February 8, 1957. After breakfast, we said goodbye to the family thanking them for their hospitality. Our gracious hostess packed sandwiches for us and our host gave Alex a small bottle of plum brandy to keep us warm in the bitter cold. Alex checked his compass and started southwest. The terrain was similar, but the ravines deeper and more frequent as we walked through the woods. The thick undergrowth slowed us down. We rested for lunch, ate our sandwiches, and we were on the move again. Alex was relentless. We lost precious time since we could not use public transportation and had to avoid people. The woods were dense, so he made frequent stops to check our course, telling us that it was easy to get lost in the woods and find ourselves walking in circles. Several times a day he offered us the plum brandy, just a swallow, to help keep us warm. I was not used to alcohol, the first little sip was a jolt and it burnt my mouth and throat, I just wanted to spit it out. Eyes watering, I thought how could anything that tasted so wretched be good for me? We continued walking.

Several times, he reminded me to eat snow. I sensed he was upset with me when he came and walked beside me. With the voice of a teacher lecturing a student he said, "I have told you repeatedly to eat snow. We do not have water, so you need to eat snow. The walking has been hard and strenuous. I do not know how much longer it will take to get to the border. Your body needs the liquid. You cannot get sick, it would complicate things."

"I am not thirsty," I protested.

"I do not want to hear any of your excuses. I know why you don't want to eat snow and I understand, but it is for your own good," he said in exasperation. I did not reply. In so many ways, I was so young. I never knew he was paying attention. Reluctantly I reached down, picked up a small handful of snow, and ate it just to satisfy him.

All too soon, walking became drudgery, up and down, in and out of ravines. The underbrush, the cold temperatures, slipping and sliding through slush and mud, wearing heavy winter coats, all contributed to slow our progress. Alex regularly checked his compass. We were often confronted with obstacles such as the huge uprooted tree that spanned a deep ravine. Should we risk a fall and walk across on the tree, or slip and slide down the ravine and climb to the other side? The trunk of the tree was wide enough for good footing, but the ravine was deep. I preferred slipping and sliding down the ravine. I was terrified of heights, but I was too embarrassed to let the rest of them know. "Are you up to it?" Alex dared us. Oddly enough, they accepted the challenge and we walked across to the other side.

The sun was setting, and very soon, it would be dark. Where would we spend the night? We continued walking. The underbrush was tick and made it more difficult to walk. Then the dense piney woods were worse, and I fumed silently, "Why did they plant trees so close together that through the years the branches intertwined?" Pushing and pulling the branches was hard work, and my arms were aching. From the ground, to way up above our heads, stood solid pine trees with not even a spot to sit down. We pressed on. Slowly the night enveloped us in darkness and cold. We could not see each other. I held my arms, in front of my face, locked in position to push away branches, and walked blindly forward. After endless minutes, I found myself stumbling slowly towards a faint tiny glow. A dim light filtered through a window of a small house. I discovered that I was standing at the edge of a clearing. Standing still, I listened and waited for the others to join me.

Without doubt, Alex was our leader, he was the only one who knew the way out of the country, and we depended upon his wisdom and experience. Yet we all knew it was not wise to walk up to a door and knock, but at the same time, I yearned, with every aching muscle, for shelter from the night. Well aware of our exhaustion, Alex was still cautious, and he whispered, "You wait here; I'll go and check the place out." He moved stealthily all around the small house before he drew near the front door and knocked. The door opened. In the doorway, we could see an elderly man. They talked briefly, and then Alex disappeared inside the house. Anxious moments later, Alex came out carrying something. He motioned us to follow him and he quickly led us to a barn connected at the end of the house. Closing the barn door behind us made it difficult to see in the darkness. Pale moonlight filtered through a small window, which helped a little. There were three stalls in the barn: one stall was directly under the window and nearest to the door, and the other two were at the opposite wall of the barn. A cow was quietly chewing her cud in the stall across the door. The others were piled high with clean straw.

As we settled down in the straw, Alex recounted his conversation with the old man who had shared his meager provisions with us. There were slices of bread and pieces of smoked bacon and we were grateful for his kindness. He offered us the use of his barn for the night. He apologized for not inviting us inside his house, but several Russian soldiers had taken up residence in his one and only bedroom. The soldiers had been out for sometime, combing the woods along the Austrian border. Usually they returned to the house before sunset and we were lucky that we had not crossed paths with them. The old man assured Alex that we would be safe in the barn, and if need be, we could hide in the straw.

After hearing all this, we ate our food in silence. Soon boisterous laughter broke the quiet, the soldiers had returned for the night. John was stretched out on the straw. Rose was sitting in a corner of the stall. I could not sit. I wanted to see what was happening in the yard. Quietly and carefully, I stood up. Leaning against the boards dividing the stalls, I could barely see out the bottom of the small window. Where I stood, I was sure they could not see me, but I had a good vantage point as I watched them go to the well, draw water, and carry the buckets into the house.

Suddenly Alex was behind me; I had not heard him move. Startled, I felt his hands on my shoulders holding me still. Slowly, deliberately, he whispered in my ear, "We are in great danger. I trust the old man, but I cannot guarantee the future. Decide now if you want to continue. At this point, I can arrange for your safe return home. John, Rose, and I can take care of ourselves. The soldiers will not take us alive. But you are my responsibility. You are the priceless treasure of your Father, my friend. I will do what is in your best interest." I felt his strong hands gripping my shoulder and then slowly moving up to encircle my neck in a tight grip. His meaning was crystal clear. I trusted him with my life. I also realized the great burden of responsibility I had placed on him. Although not of his choosing, he had accepted the responsibility. His grip tightened around my neck, and his voice was flat, "They will not take you alive. Knowing what would happen to you, I could not live with that burden. If I cannot protect you, I will have to take your life." Motionless, we stood there for a long time.

His warning echoed in my mind. The lights flickered off in the house and all was in darkness. When he thought I had sufficient time to think it over, he asked, "What have you decided?"

I answered, "I am not going back."

He wrapped his arms around me, holding me tight, softly said, "I hope I did not make a mistake bringing you along." Decision made and consequences understood, he sat and rested beside his beloved Rose. I found a spot in the straw, wrapped my coat around me and leaned against the wall. I did not dare to fall asleep.

Come daybreak it was good to see light filtering through the window. I wanted to be far, far away from this place. I felt trapped in the barn. The woods had appeared safer, at least until now. Alex waited for the soldiers to leave first. He knew they were searching the woods to the west and we were heading southwest. Even if it took longer, he made sure our paths would not cross. Checking his compass, we started out. These woods were easier to walk in, with less and less underbrush and no more pine trees. It was very cold and a thin layer of snow covered the ground making the crossing of deep ravines an ordeal. We were on a forced march and rarely rested. Alex was determined to make better time. He was on target. He knew where we were and we needed to reach Davidhaza, a small village, before dark. I often thought resentfully, "If only the terrain would cooperate!" In late afternoon, we reached a small stream, swollen with melted snow. While trying to find a good spot to cross, we soon learned we did not have any choice. We stepped into the ice-cold water and started to cross. The water washed over the top of my shoe and filled it, sending chills through my entire body. It kept rising higher. Soon it was up to my knees. My teeth were chattering. By force of will, I made my legs rise since I could no longer feel my feet. At last, we staggered to the other side. We had no change of clothes and no time to build a fire to dry them. We had to continue.

The hours passed, it was getting late, the sun was setting, and we were still freezing. Soon darkness would descend; the night air was cold, and no sign of Davidhaza. Mind and body had one goal, keep moving. Many footsteps later, we saw plowed farmland ahead. We were out of the forest. Plowed farmlands meant a village nearby. Soon, darkness like a blanket covered us. Alex was pleased, no one could see us arrive in the village. Even in the darkness he knew exactly where he was going. He found the house, fenced in with a high wooden fence to ensure the privacy of the owner, and tried the gate. It opened easily, we walked through it into the yard.

We tried to clean the dirt and mud from our shoes before knocking on the door. The owner, hearing the noise on the porch, opened the door to investigate. With the light from the open door shining on us, he immediately recognized Alex. He urged us inside to a warm kitchen where several curious faces looked us over. His wife, with their two young children, and the elderly parents of his wife, were relaxing after their supper. The elderly couple took notice of our pitiful condition and insisted, "Take your coats off, you are soaking wet. Come close to the fire and warm up." We did not need any more encouragement, stripping our frozen pants and shoes off, we handed them to the old couple. The old woman brought a small blanket and wrapped it around my legs, and pushed me to sit by the fire. That dear old man took our wet and muddy shoes, cleaned them, rubbed them with some kind of grease, filled them with grain, and set them by the fire, all the while telling me that the grain would soak up the moisture and the grease would keep the leather from drying out.

Alex, John and the man were in deep conversation, while Rose and I were made very comfortable by this dear family. The young mother was warming up the leftover soup, making scrambled eggs, potatoes, fried sausage, and anything she could gather on short notice to provide dinner for us. It touched me deeply to be a recipient of such gracious hospitality. The men talked late into the night, but Rose and I were shown into the bedroom where she and I shared a bed and Alex and John the other.

Sunday morning, February 10, 1957, we awoke to a cold but sunny, pleasant day. The aroma of breakfast cooking drifted into the bedroom. We rose and got ready. Our travel stained clothes and shoes were dry and clean. This was the day, the day we had been waiting for with such great anticipation. We went into the kitchen where the family was waiting to serve us. That kind grandmother sat beside me, urging me to eat, solicitous of my well-being. This dear family wanted our last experience in Hungary to be a memorable one. The young mother packed us a lunch for the road. It was time for us to say good-bye.

Early Sunday morning the streets were almost deserted. It did not take long to walk through the little village. Soon we found ourselves out in the farm country. As far as our eyes could see stretched a vast expanse of plowed fields and open land. We felt vulnerable. Alex did not have to remind us to scan the horizon and keep a watchful eye for vehicles en route to the border. If we could see them, they could see us. We did not use the easy country road; instead, we tramped through the fields. He reminded us repeatedly to be alert and if we noticed anything suspicious to drop to the ground immediately, and do not move. . We did not linger, walking our last steps on Hungarian soil, but kept marching at as fast a pace as we could maintain. The wet soil of the plowed fields stuck to our shoes and added weight to already tired legs.

After several hours of walking, we found a dry irrigation ditch. We descended into the ditch, sat down to rest our sore legs and ate our well-deserved lunch. We rested for about an hour while Alex briefed us about what we could expect at the border. During our conversation, I mentioned that we did not know the names of the three families who gave us shelter along the way, and that he was the only one who knew. He smiled and said, "You do not need to know, it is best they remain anonymous." We were eager to be on our way, but before we climbed out of the ditch, we made sure it was safe.

Of the four days we had to walk, this one was the most nerve-wracking. Alex encouraged us, "Keep walking, if all goes according to plan, we'll cross over into Yugoslavia during the night." Never a word of complaint passed our lips no matter how hard or difficult the day was. As a unit, we focused on our mission—escaping from Hungary safely. At last, the sun was setting. Once again Alex checked his compass and his hand pointed out the way. Dimly, in the distance, we could glimpse the outline of woods in the direction we were heading. It was dark by the time we reached them. Alex was watching the sky. The full moon was shining brightly, but we could see clouds moving in. We all hoped for a cloudy dark night. During the day, we talked and laughed to ease our tension. Now, Alex reminded us to be quiet, voices carry in the night. We were silent as we entered the woods. There were twigs and leaves under our feet and he reminded us to step carefully. I considered, how could I be careful, when I could not even see where I stepped? We walked four abreast with an arm length of distance between us. We were slowly and quietly plodding in the darkness when the sound of barking dogs froze us to the spot. We did not move, yet my rapid heart-beat was pounding so loudly in my ears I was sure it could be heard. We knew we were in the border area, not exactly sure how far, but this entire area was patrolled. Hyper alert, with ears and eyes straining, we listened and waited. The sound of voices and the barking of the dogs were getting closer. In the pale moonlight, just ahead of us, we could barely distinguish the outline of the group. A small group of soldiers and two dogs were on patrol approximately fifty feet from us. Breathless, I stood staring eyes wide; fearful the dogs would pick up our scent. Motionless, we watched as they swaggered by. We stood there for a long time, just in case, wanting to be safe before we started walking once again. Soon we crossed the path where the soldiers had walked. We continued cautiously and then discovered a small depression in the ground filled with a dense growth of shrubs, and we halted. We crouched down under the shrubs for protection. With few words, Alex explained his dire plan. Rose and I were to remain hidden in the shrubs while he and John scouted out the area. They would return for us in about an hour, but no later than an hour and a half. In the event they would not return, we had to leave the area and try to make it on our own.

Without uttering a word, we watched as the two men quickly disappeared into the darkness and then we settled back, listening, watching, and waiting. I looked at my watch. It was 8:00 pm. If they did not return by 9:30 pm, we were on our own. The clouds moved in and covered the full moon, what a relief. The air felt as though it could rain any time. We waited, and waited, with all our senses on high alert. Sitting there, I realized how hard it was to wait. While time slowed to a crawl, my thoughts churned, each passing quickly, but all filled with trepidation and worry. Ever since that first step from home, I had told myself repeatedly, do not think, just do as they do. I must not become a burden, I must not let them down, and I must not let my emotions betray us to the enemy. I desperately did not want to think. Moving kept emotions and thoughts at bay, but now I could not ignore long suppressed feelings and fears. I had time to reflect. My stomach was a hard knot and my body trembled. Too much had happened and too fast to absorb and process it all. I knew Alex and John had been tortured by the secret police, yet they were calm, focused, and quiet. As I concentrated on the silent and composed woman beside me, I found comfort and reassurance.

Rose was a strong woman. If we had to, surely we could make it on our own. I sensed her fear, not for herself, but for Alex. Would she have the strength to cross the border without him? She knew better than I what would happen to him if he was captured again. Knowing this, and loving him so, could she leave him? Time dragged on, after endless minutes, the hour finally passed by, still no sight of the men. If I thought the first hour was hard to endure, the next minutes were nigh unbearable. We had come so far, and now were so close to the border; would we be caught while escape was almost within our grasp? I watched as the clock hands approached 9:30, and then pass. I was silent, waiting for her decision. She was still. Finally, Rose lifted my arm to check the time. It was 9:45 pm. What could have happened? Where were they? What should we do? How long would Rose wait? A sound filtered through my anxious thoughts, footsteps were close by. Torn between hope and fear, we did not move; had the border patrol returned?

We nearly cried with joy, what a relief it was to hear the soft voice of Alex.

With great haste, we rejoined the men and started walking again. Before long, we were out of the woods. Stretching ahead before us, as far as we could see with our limited visibility, were plowed fields. During the day, the temperature warmed to above freezing and the melted snow thawed the ground and turned the field into soft mud. Walking in the soft mud was excruciating. Every step was an effort as our feet sunk deep in the mud. Pulling them out made a loud noise. The gooey mud collected around our shoes, and without a Herculean effort to keep them on, would have pulled them off. I knew we must be quiet, but how could we be quiet in this field when every step created a roaring sound? We slogged through the mud, lifting a leg that felt heavier with every step.

Far ahead in the distance, we could see lights shining through some windows. Alex whispered that it was an outpost for soldiers. I was stunned. What was he thinking? He was leading us right by those buildings. What if the dogs should hear us, or some of the soldiers see us? They had to be deaf not to hear the noise we were making. My feet trudged ahead but my head was turned in the direction of the houses. While I tried to keep an eye in both directions, I needed to keep up with the others and not fall behind.

Suddenly, something long and high stretched out in front of us creating a barrier. Peering into the darkness, I wondered, what could this be? Getting closer, we recognized railroad tracks, elevated higher than the boggy ground around them. It towered above us and we had no choice but to crawl up the gravel sides. We made so much noise it sounded like an avalanche in the silent night. Scrambling up through the loose gravel, we laid flat on our stomachs on top of the tracks, eyes searching to see what was on the other side. We could not see anything in that dark, desolate, no-man's-land, as far as our eye could see. I looked down and saw stars reflected in the water. My heart pounded with exertion and fear until I was nearly breathless.

Resolutely, Alex said, "Let's go." So we slid down the other side of the tracks with as much noise as before and landed into the water with a splash. I was relieved the water did not wash over my muddy shoes. We kept walking and staring, walking and staring, our heads spinning in every direction. Every shrub that stuck out of the water looked like a soldier. It had been almost four hours since our encounter with the soldiers on patrol. How much longer would we have to wander in this desolate no-man's-land? We were in an area where they shoot first and ask questions later. Fear, with its icy fingers, gripped my soul and my heart was beating in my throat. Soundlessly my mind repeated, "What if? What if?" followed by, "Don't think, walk!" as I mechanically put one foot in front of the other. For us to ever get out of this mess, we would need God's help. It had been years since I said my prayers. I was rummaging around in my mind trying to find a suitable prayer for such a situation and could not find even one. Even if I did, who knows how long it would take a saint to intercede for us? We needed help now! The only prayer I knew addressed directly to God was the Lord's Prayer. Did I dare to pray that? Would God even hear it? These were desperate times, so I recited, "Our Father which art in heaven, Hallowed be Thy name..." this is as far as I got. I knew the entire prayer, but I kept repeating the same line over and over again, not sure, if God even heard it. First mud, now water, we splashed ahead as fast as our footing permitted. We pressed on, eyes searching rapidly for any signs of the border or of soldiers on patrol, eventually I realized that we were no longer walking in water, but on soundless grass.

In the distance, we could see barbed wire, our first sign of the border. The minefield! I remembered hearing horror stories about the minefields in front of the border. Such a ghastly method of ensuring no one escapes. At the same time, I heard John ask the same question. Alex replied, "There are no mines out there." What? How could he know that? What did he mean, no mines out there? I remembered his admonition, no questions, but this was one time I was sorely tried. A barbed wire fence of six to eight feet in height stretched along the border delineating the territory of the entire country. The barbed wire fence ahead of us was rusty and old. In some places it had been removed and rolled into a bundle. It would not prevent anyone from crossing it, unlike the one on the Austrian border. We carefully passed through the loose barbed wire into the clay field. This area was approximately six to eight feet wide and paralleled the barbed wire fence along the border. As we stepped across the soft clay, we left our footprints behind clear for all to see, highly visible marks of four escaping Hungarians. At the edge of the clay field ran a narrow two feet wide shallow ditch, marking the actual border. We stepped across it and started to run. We ran as hard and fast as we could. I could feel my lungs screaming for air and my chest hurt but we kept on running. Finally, Alex stopped and breathlessly we all huddled together hugging each other. As soon as I could, I looked at my watch and announced it was midnight. It started to rain. After six danger filled days and many harrowing experiences, we had made it. We were free! We were free!

We crossed over into Yugoslavia, just as Alex had planned at the tri border area near Hodos.

We huddled in the rain, silent, preoccupied with our own private thoughts, waiting for Alex to lead. How do I say thank you to God? Out here in the rain, it seemed inappropriate. He was the Almighty God who lived in churches. It had to be a proper thank you. Maybe, one day it would be.

FIRST STEPS TO FREEDOM

Alex's voice brought me out of my reverie. "Let's go. We do not have to run, but we have to be alert. The Yugoslavs have border guards also. There is a farmhouse a few kilometers from here, and I know the people living there."

An hour or so of walking, I could see the faint outline of a building in the distance. It was a solitary house, no fence, no gates, just a large building in the middle of the fields. A solid wood door protected the inner door and the shutters on the windows were tightly closed, providing a shield against the harsh elements and some security. Alex pounded on the door and waited. We heard the grumbling of a man as he opened the doors and peered out in the darkness. Alex stood by the door and as soon as it was opened, he greeted his friend. In the next minutes, we witnessed the joyous reunion of two friends embracing in a huge bear hug. The man repeated over and over again, "Alex, it's just like old times! When I heard of your capture, I gave up hope of ever seeing you again. Come in, come in."

He soon noticed Alex was not alone and invited the rest of us to follow him through an entryway into a warm kitchen where his wife, obviously awakened from sleep and wrapped in a robe, was waiting to see who was escorted into her home. Her husband, with arms around Alex, called to her in joyous exclamations to announce their visitor. Jumping to her feet, she embraced Alex and cried out, "Alex! Just like old times! Let me look at you. What have they done to you?" Their reunion was touching.

The man was tall and thin, but there was a strength about him. With his hair graying at the temples, he was probably in his fifties. His wife, also tall and slender, had a beautiful gentle face and eyes filled with warmth and kindness. Her thick hair was pulled up in a bun. It was obvious that they were a part of the network of men and women Alex knew in his line of work. Once again, I noticed that as we were introduced to the family, Alex did not reveal their names. We removed our wet coats and the woman offered us hot tea and rolls. The three men were deep in conversation. I was exhausted and could barely keep my eyes open. Now that we had crossed the border, the past events had truly caught up with me. The woman was urging, "Let me get you to bed, poor child. You are worn out." Putting her arms around me, she led me to the bedroom and tucked me in. Her gentle and kind ways made me feel so welcome. Soon I was sound asleep.

The next thing I heard was loud voices from the kitchen waking me up. What time was it? It cannot be morning! I could not keep my eyes open. I felt I had just fallen asleep and could sleep for days. My next surprise was hearing Rose beside me inquiring, "What's going on? What time is it?" I was sleeping so deeply I never heard her arrive. Alex, fully dressed, walked in the bedroom, and answered her question. "It is five in the morning, and two Yugoslav border guards are waiting in the kitchen to talk to us." We dressed quickly and joined them in the kitchen.

The guards were not friendly. They did not give us time to eat the simple breakfast prepared for us. Thoughts tumbled in my sleepy mind. I knew they were doing their job, but couldn't they have waited a little longer to let us sleep and then eat? How did they ever find out where we were? Where were they taking us? They escorted us to their jeep and ordered us to get in. They did not speak Hungarian, but all four of us understood most of what they were saying. They spoke in a Slavic dialect, which was very similar to Russian. Three hours later, around eight o'clock in the morning, they stopped at a police station where, through an interpreter, they interrogated us, asking all types of questions such as where did we cross and why were we in their country? They demanded to see our identification cards. We were detained at this station for couple of hours while they deliberated what to do with us. One of the soldiers brought in a plate of hard rolls. I was so hungry I ate one.

I am sure the soldiers reported our presence in their country to their superiors, and they must have received some orders that dictated their next action. Two of the soldiers returned and then drove us to a railroad station. Boarding the train, the soldiers sat across from us. Obviously, we were under guard until we reached our destination. Before Alex took his seat, he whispered, "Whatever you do, don't dare to fall asleep." The rhythmic rolling of the train was putting me to sleep. We could not talk because the soldiers wanted us to be quiet. My body was unwinding; I was sleepy, since I only had about three hours of sleep. To keep awake, I considered instead where were they taking us. Finally the train stopped. The soldiers rose to their feet and motioned for us to follow. The sign over the station read, Radenzi. It was a center to process refugees entering Yugoslavia.

My first step toward freedom led to a refugee camp. The soldiers escorted us to an office, turned us over to the authorities and left. From what I could observe, the camp was administered by the Yugoslav secret service soldiers along with humanitarian agencies including the Red

Cross. Once again, the secret service questioned us individually. Just as before, I gave the same information. I had no secrets, nothing to hide, so I gave honest answers. I was waiting in a small lobby when I was called back into the office. I had no idea why. Alex was sitting there with the same officer engaged in a friendly conversation. Because I was a minor, Alex was appointed as my guardian. Later Alex shared with us that several of his friends were administering some of the refugee camps around Yugoslavia. He was among friends. I received stationary, stamps, and I wrote to my parents of our safe arrival. I also sent a letter to my aunt and uncle in the United States.

The camp was crowded, and they were trying to find places for us to stay. Alex and Rose shared a large room with married couples, John a room with single men, and I a room with single women. This was a temporary situation until they could find places for us in the various refugee camps. The next few days were busy; we had physicals and forms to complete. We were asked to name the country of our choice that we would like to immigrate to, and the names of relatives or contacts there. I listed the United States.

Settling in my assigned room, the women pointed to the shower room in another building. It was pure pleasure to shower and clean up after a week of tracking through the woods. Unhappily, I had to put on the same clothes; I had hoped that somehow I could wash my garments. Living in a dorm prepared me to share a large room with strangers so I was used to the lack of privacy. The meals were served in large dining halls. I joined Alex, Rose, and John for all our meals. I was hungry and tired; the last few days were taking their toll. Shortly after dinner, I went to bed.

Early the following morning I discovered that either the military or the dean of my dorm ran the camp, when I heard bell announcing it was time to get up. We had to quickly clean up, dress, make our beds, and tidy the room to be ready for the morning inspection before breakfast. I fully understood the reason. Cleanliness was of utmost importance to prevent disease and infection from spreading among so many people living in close quarters.

Alex spent long hours talking with his friend John. I was curious and wanted to know so much about his experiences, but he was reluctant to share them. Occasionally he would reminisce about some of their narrow escapes crossing the borders. I had the opportunity to meet four of the daredevil men who risked their lives for the cause they believed in. They were multilingual, fluent in several languages. These men shared a strong bond of friendship. I was also learning more and more about my childhood friend and his wife Rose. Their love endured separations, danger, imprisonment, and torture before, at long last they were able to start over in freedom.

Our stay in Radenzi was brief, and then we were relocated to another camp in Stattenberg, in the Slovenian mountains. The setting was beautiful with mountains, forests and lakes, and we could leave the camp and walk around in the woods. I wondered what would happen to me; I felt my life was on hold in a waiting pattern. I continued writing to my parents and relatives, keeping them informed. My aunt and uncle, whom I had never met, assured me that they were eager to welcome me into their home and to do everything possible to make my stay in the camps short.

At Stattenberg, I shared a small room with six other women. We received some articles of much needed clothing. With so many of us living in close quarters, we soon were making new friends, getting acquainted, sharing our experiences and our hopes of starting out in a new country. One of the women in our room was a doctor who was going to the Congo to study tropical diseases. She had all her papers in order and was just waiting to hear the time of her departure. One morning I woke up very sick with a burning fever. She noticed right away that something was wrong. After telling her my symptoms, she said I had a full-blown kidney infection. She had nothing to treat me with, was leaving in two days, so she told me to drink a lot of water. I could not stay in bed so I forced myself to go downstairs, join Alex and the gang for meals, and pretend I was fine. I made many excuses for visiting the restroom and this made Rose suspicious. I was miserable, and I remembered Alex's reminders of eating snow. It took almost three weeks before I was feeling better.

The smaller camps were closing and once again, we were relocated to another camp. Our first separation came when they moved all the single men to another location. John was the first to leave our little band. We had always been together and shared a close bond of friendship. We knew he was troubled. Rose and I tried to reassure him that it would be fine, even though we did not know what would happen to any of us. The bus pulled up in front of our camp and we had to say good-bye. It was hard since we had no guarantee of ever seeing each other again. I was sincerely hoping that he would make it to his relatives in Canada. As we stood there waving to him as long as we could see the bus, I remembered his painful good-bye to his parents. Would we always have to say good-bye to those we love?

The following week I was informed that it was my turn to leave for a camp in Brestanica. I knew from painful personal experience that people we did not know, and events we did not plan, would be in control of our lives. I was brave as I hugged Rose and Alex good-bye. Now I was alone with no one to watch over me. I had to be responsible, stand-alone and remember all that I was taught by my parents. Sitting on the crowded bus feeling all alone was a sobering experience. The bus traveled through some beautiful countryside. We drove down by the Sava River and up to the mountaintop. We arrived at a massive old building and the huge gates swung open to let us inside the courtyard. It was an ancient monastery situated on a mountaintop with a magnificent view. Refugees clustered around the bus ready to greet the new arrivals. I was assigned to a room with twenty women of all ages. We looked for those near our own age. It was easy to make new friends, even though we knew it would not be a lasting friendship, for soon we would be scattered all over the world. We could explore the monastery and the mountains and caves around it. We were told that Marshal Tito and his partisans fought in these mountains and hid in the caves. It was a wonderful lesson in history knowing that they defeated the Nazis.

All the camps I stayed in were closely guarded by the Yugoslav military. We had limited freedom; we were only permitted to explore our immediate surroundings. We had a regimented routine to follow each day, including keeping our rooms, common areas, and the grounds clean. At several times in the different camps, we had visitors from the Red Cross and other humanitarian groups from all over the world, to ensure that we had reasonably adequate housing and food. Toiletries were given out regularly. We became accustomed to the communal showers and restrooms.

Every week busloads of refugees were arriving and we always met the bus to greet the new arrivals. It was at such an occasion that I saw Rose and Alex getting off the bus. It was pure happiness to see them, and a week later brought another surprise. John was getting off the bus. He was so happy to see us. What a great reunion!

Alex became very sick at Brestanica. Fortunately, another one of his friends was the director of this camp. I was no longer surprised at meeting his friends in all sorts of places. When it became apparent Alex needed to be hospitalized, his friend arranged for him to be sent to a nearby hospital. Alex had endured unbelievable torture at that house of terror on Andrassy Boulevard in Budapest, and it caused permanent damage to his internal organs. Weeks later, he returned to the refugee camp and I would visit him. He told me that as soon as he was able, he and Rose would be leaving for Belgium, the country of their choice. I was happy for them. I had not heard anything about my leaving for the States. Regularly, delegations from different countries would visit our camps and invite us to their countries. I could have gone to Australia, Switzerland,

Germany, France, or Holland. There were so many choices and tempting offers, but my dream was to go to America.

It was the middle of summer and I was still waiting. I continued regular correspondence with family and relatives. Mother wrote that she had a letter from the parents of Edith and Nicholas and that they had extended their invitation for me to live with them in Germany. She urged me to accept their offer; at least I would remain on the same continent. I thought it was very kind of them to offer, but no thank you. A cold chill ran through me as I recalled Edith's drawing of death and her unkind spirit. I knew I would go anywhere but there.

Many of the refugees were leaving Brestanica to depart to the country of their choice. There were hundreds of young people under the age of twenty-one in the various refugee camps. We were relocated to Bela-Crkva, a camp for minors. When I said good-bye to Alex, Rose, and John, I knew it would be our final good-bye. While in Bela–Crkva, I heard from Mother that Rose and Alex had made it to Belgium. I never heard from them personally. I fervently wished that somehow John had made it to Canada.

Bela-Crkva was located close to the Romanian border. Ironically, we crossed into Yugoslavia at the western most part of that country, and throughout the year, I traveled across the country staying at various refugee camps.

The girls were housed in an orphanage for Greek children at one end of this village, the boys at the opposite end in a makeshift military camp. The man who supervised the girls' camp was the director of the orphanage. The orphans were in summer camp and we used their facilities in their absence. The director of the boys' camp, whose name I had heard several times during the past months, was none other than Alex's friend, the mastermind of all their operations. While staying at this refugee camp, every Sunday afternoon we walked to the movies to see the heroic exploits of Marshall Tito and his partisans.

The food at these camps was adequate, but growing teenagers needed a more nutritional and balanced diet. I felt weaker by the day and it was difficult to walk. I had to sit down and rest frequently. Twenty-four of us shared a bedroom and there were over one hundred girls in this camp. Our room was on the second floor and it became an effort to walk the stairs. Every other step I had to sit down and rest. Susan, my closest friend was concerned. My skin looked yellow. One day, I made it down the stairs and sat on the steps outside the door. Resting there, I watched the girls play ball. I wanted to join them, but I had no strength to stand up. We were accustomed to seeing foreign guests regularly visiting the camp. Our camp director was showing a group of French doctors around the camp. I sat on the steps and watched them go by. I noticed one of the doctors looking at me intently. He passed by, turned around, and stopped to look at me again. He said something to the nurse who was the interpreter. The nurse came and told me the doctor wanted to have my blood checked and would I please walk with her to the local doctor's office? A healthy person could have made the trip in less than ten minutes. It took us almost forty-five minutes. The old village doctor examined me and told me in broken Hungarian that he would draw blood to be tested. I sat on an old solid wood chair, held my arm out to him and he prepared it to draw blood. He was not even finished when I felt very hot, my head spinning. I had millions of colored dots flashing through my eyes, and then oblivion. Finally, I came to and heard the doctor and nurse talking to me, gently shaking my arm to wake me up. The doctor informed the nurse that I was severely anemic, in fact, dangerously so. The nurse held her arm around my waist, supporting me, as with many faltering steps we walked back to the camp. She helped me straight back to the clinic at the orphanage, and put me in bed.

I was so weak I could not lift up my arms. I was floating in and out of consciousness. When I closed my eyes, I felt as if I was looking into a kaleidoscope with hundreds of brilliant colored circles and dots floating in midnight black space. When I tried to sit up or raise my head, I became dizzy and the inside of my head felt hot and I floated into oblivion. My friends would visit me and sit near me on my bed. I knew they were there but I could not respond to them. I felt as if I was living in another world, a kind of twilight zone, weightless, floating in space.

The camp director made daily visits checking my condition and encouraging me to eat. I could not even look at food, let alone eat it. The village doctor made his visits too. He new only a few words in Hungarian, but he would make an effort to put a sentence together to talk to me. I knew he did not know how bad his morning greetings sounded. "You, poor blood, every day I come, I think you are gone, you look so dead." It would have been an unsettling greeting, to say the least, if I had not looked into the kind and gentle face of this elderly doctor and seen the concern in his eyes.

Shortly after the French doctor's visit, the clinic received a box of medication to treat me. I needed to drink a vial of this brown bad tasting liquid in a small glass of water every morning and evening. The nurse warned me that I had an iron deficiency, a folic acid deficiency, and a number of other things that I did not understand, and that this would help me. I drank the potion faithfully. Many weeks later, I knew I was improving; the multi-color circles and dots were disappearing and I was no longer lightheaded, except if I got up quickly. The village doctor's visits became less frequent. I could return to my room and only visited the clinic to take my medicine.

Summer was over and the Greek orphans were returning from their summer camp, it was time to move again. While letters from relatives and family were frequent, and a comfort, waiting was increasingly difficult, since I could not help but notice how many of the refugees had already left. When would it be my turn? My friend, Susan, and I were both headed for the States. She had relatives in Wheeling, West Virginia, and I in Akron, Ohio.

We were relocated to a small village named Ecka. This would be our final refugee camp. From this camp, we would be transported to our final destination. At this camp, we had physicals and all kinds of shots, preparing us for departure. As children, we were already immunized against most diseases and could not understand why we needed the shots again. We were finger printed, had our pictures taken and stood before numbers of delegations from various countries and organizations answering myriads of questions. Then we waited.

Our food supply was limited. Those in the kitchen would literally dump baskets of sliced bread on long tables. We searched to find some that were not dry or moldy. As in all previous camps, we were guarded by soldiers. The camp resembled a military boot camp with barracks laid out like a small village. Each barrack housed about thirty people. The only difference was, at this camp we were all thrown together; married, singles, males, females and families with children. Susan and I were assigned to different barracks; we were very disappointed since we had hoped to stay together. With so much uncertainty in our lives, it was a comfort to share and be near a friend. Our daily routine was regimented. Rooms were inspected every morning to make sure all living areas were clean. Each day someone from the camp would make the rounds and leave five cigarettes on all the beds, regardless of the age of the occupant. At first, I would give my share to anyone in the room who smoked, but as time went by, Susan and I realized that the cigarettes had great bartering power in the nearby village. Almost every day, we would escape from the camp to visit the local village. In the previous camps, we were allowed some freedom to leave the camp. Here in Ecka we were not. It was a military camp and the entire area was fenced in with barbed wire. Since we were not allowed to leave through the front gate, we crawled through the fence in the back. After the morning routine was over, Susan and I would gather up all kinds of things we could barter for food in the village, including the cigarettes we hoarded from the previous days.

Our first stop was the home of the family whose back-yard we used for a shortcut. Four generations of a gypsy family lived there. They were friendly, engaging us in conversation, and curious about what we had to trade. This family always had the first choice of the spoils for trading. Without fail, the matriarch of the clan had a bottle of milk waiting for us, which we drank immediately. Refreshed we continued on our exploration of the village. One of the women stopped us on the street and invited us in for lunch. She did not want anything from us, she recognized that we were refugees and extended her hospitality. We became their regular guests. Later, we discovered she was the wife of the mayor of this village. She invited us for a Sunday dinner so her entire family could meet us. We met several families in this small village. We had breakfast with the gypsies, lunch with another family and dinner at the mayor's.

Several of our roommates knew of our visits to the village and they gave us all kinds of things so we could barter for such things as eggs and milk for them. At various times while in the camp, we were given canned foods. Some needed to be cooked when opened and since we had no means of cooking, they became an item to trade. We received many cans of scallops that we could not use. Even our roommates gave them to us. We supplied this little village with so many cans that the mayor's wife protested, "Please do not bring me any more."

Located approximately twenty kilometers from Ecka was a small Hungarian town. This area, prior to the war, was part of Hungary, and after the division of territories became a part of Yugoslavia. Susan and I decided it was close enough to visit. We started early in the morning and by noon we were in this little town talking with a clerk in a store. She invited us to go home with her and meet her parents. We became very close to this family and spent a lot of time with them. Three other families in this town "adopted" us. We did not mind the walk or the distance; we had a wonderful time enjoying the hospitality of these kind families.

Winter was fast approaching. It was cold and the barracks had no heat. The men found several fifty-gallon drums and rigged up a heating system. We just had to find fuel, so the hunt began. A resourceful person discovered a storage shed at camp, full of coal and solved that problem. Because of the cold, our trips to the villages were infrequent. Asiatic flu hit the camp. We were miserable with high fever and body aches. We stayed in bed hoping it would pass. Meanwhile, buses were shuttling refugees to the airport in Belgrade, leaving for destinations around the world. Those of us desiring to go to America were waiting and hoping that our turn would come soon. I had arrived in Yugoslavia on February 10, 1957, and now it was December 10, 1957, and I was still waiting.

Meanwhile, in Akron, Ohio, Uncle Michael and Aunt Julia were anxious to find out what was happening. He even purchased airline tickets and sent them to Yugoslavia, paying for my airfare. They had every intention of supporting me and assuming full responsibility in providing for my needs. Uncle Michael was retired and worked part time at the Portage Country Club. Many of the employees and members knew he wanted to bring me to the States and they offered their support and encouragement. The treasurer of the Country Club frequently inquired about my situation. Uncle Michael expressed his frustration of not being able to do anything to speed up the process. The treasurer informed my Uncle that there would be a dinner at the Club and Congressman George Ayers would be the guest speaker. He asked if Uncle had a recent picture of me, and would he be willing to give it to him. The treasurer knew someone influential attending the dinner and he asked this person to talk with the Congressman to see if he could expedite matters. The Congressman graciously agreed, and because of his clout, I was scheduled to come to America.

During this time, I was unaware of all the events that transpired and the arrangements made for my departure. All I knew was, at last, my name was on the list of passengers to board the bus transporting us to Belgrade and to the airport. It was so hard to believe that my time had finally come and I was indeed going to America. It was a dream come true.

GOING TO AMERICA

We boarded a four-propeller airplane and I chose a seat at the window, watching the man on the ground turn the propellers by hand to get them started. One by one, the propellers were twirling around and around. Wedges were removed from the tires. The roar of the engines was deafening. The plane started to move and before long, we were airborne. What a wonderful feeling, my first flight. It was the beginning of a new life. I was facing an unknown future, but it was my future, one that I chose for myself.

From Belgrade, we flew to Ireland and arrived there in the late afternoon. The flight attendant notified us that we would be served dinner there. We were directed to a beautiful dining room with tables set with white linens, crystal glassware, and china fit for a king. The people of Ireland, in our honor, prepared this wonderful setting and feast for our enjoyment. Here we were, hungry, weary, ragged refugees, seated at this banquet, individually served by waiters dressed in black suits with white napkins draped over their arms, anticipating our every need. Their kindness and courtesy was overwhelming. As a child, I was taught proper table manners so sitting at this table was not an awkward experience. At the refugee camps, we were one of the masses trying to survive. By contrast, the staff at the airport and those in Ireland treated us with respect. They did not see our shabby appearance. They looked beyond and saw the individual.

After dinner, we returned to our plane and continued our journey. We flew all night. Occasionally the pilot would tell us to look down and see the lights of the cities. The following day we landed in New Foundland and had breakfast there. We sat around this huge oval shaped diner counter and the waitress served us a big breakfast. They prepared a small treat of oranges, apples, and candy to eat on the plane later.

On December 19, 1957, we landed at La Guardia airport in New York. Before landing, the flight attendant suggested that we eat our snack because we would not be allowed to take it into the airport. We were instructed as to what to expect going through customs and immigration. The airport and customs were a blur. There were so many people everywhere and moving fast. We did not have time to look around but followed the person in charge leading us through the maze. All this took a long time. It was dark when we boarded the bus taking us to our hotel. On the way we gazed with amazement at the skyscrapers and the sights along the streets. The interpreter pointed out the Statue of Liberty in the distance. It was dark and the driver was not taking us on a sight seeing tour. We barely glanced at the famous statue welcoming the huddled masses, yearning to be free.

We arrived in the Bronx in front of the Saint George Hotel. Again, we lined up single file and followed our guide and the interpreter. The staff had everything organized as they ushered us through various rooms. Presenting our identification cards, we moved from room to room. At one station, we received a key to our room and at the next station packages of toiletries and pajamas. The staff was very efficient at their job; they hardly looked at us as they performed their duties. We in turn followed the person in front of us as the guide led us through the rooms. Finally, we were in the lobby holding our gift packages and our room keys. I did not know any of the people traveling with me on the airplane, so a woman in her thirties was assigned the same room with me.

We waited for the elevator to take us to our floor. The elevator door opened and we stepped inside. I turned to look for the control panel. There in the corner of the elevator, next to the control panel, stood a very tall young Negro man, smiling. He was so tall I had to look up to see his face. He had a great big smile on his face and a beautiful set of white teeth as he spoke in Hungarian, "Welcome to America." I realized I was staring. Embarrassed at my poor manners, I returned his smile, holding out my key for him to see. He was the first person of his race I had ever seen. He must have known this, because for several months many of the Hungarian refugees were processed through his hotel. Of all the people we had met who directed us thus far, this young man was the first person who welcomed us to America. He took the time to learn the difficult Hungarian language so he could talk to us and help us during those first days of our stay. Our room was on the twenty-eighth floor. On our short ride up, he was teaching us to say "twenty-eight" in English.

Settled in our room, it was wonderful to soak in a hot tub of water. I put on my new pajamas, but I could not go to sleep. My roommate was sound asleep while I stared out the window looking at the illuminated buildings, my heart so full of mixed emotions. While I was in Yugoslavia, even though I was living in refugee camps, I felt I was close to home. Here, so far away from everyone I loved and knew, I was very alone.

New

Life

PART 4

FIRST IMPRESSIONS

On my second day in New York, I wandered outside to explore the city. I knew the cities of Europe but New York City was different. The streets were crowded with people hurrying and rushing. The sights and sounds were unfamiliar. The store windows displayed beautiful clothes, shoes, and coats. Jewelry stores looked like treasure chests filled with gold, silver, and precious stones. I had arrived a few days before Christmas. It seemed that every store competed to have the most spectacular Christmas display in their windows. Store windows were filled to overflowing with toys of every description. I had never seen such an abundant display of things to satisfy the wildest imagination of a human heart. People were pushing by, rushing and hardly glancing at the breathtaking displays in the store windows. I could not stop walking. I was looking and staring, my senses were overwhelmed. I could hardly take in the sights. Some of the store windows held objects I had never seen and could not imagine what they were.

Strolling down the street of this wonderland, I realized it was getting late. I forgot time and distance. I had to return to the hotel. I remained on the same side of the street, even though I had walked a long distance. New York City was huge. The entire population of Hungary could fit inside it. I had an unsettling feeling that I could get lost here very easily. I did not speak the language. I had to be more careful, this was not Hungary, nor Yugoslavia. A clock in the store window reminded me that I had walked almost three hours. I would have to hurry to find my way back before dark. I had an exhilarating adventure in this grand new world.

The following day I was transferred to Hoboken, New Jersey, to travel to Akron. The train station was enormous. I was beginning to understand that everything in this new world was on a grand scale. An escort, who did not speak Hungarian, accompanied me to the train and to my assigned seat. He introduced me to the conductor. He left me in his care to take me safely to Akron. My escort gave me $5.00 to purchase anything I might need along the way. My ticket was in a small envelope, on the cover was a map listing some of the cities along the way. Following the map, I assumed that I would arrive in Akron in a short time. I sat by the window and spent the time comparing the names of the cities we passed with the ones on the envelope. I realized that we were passing too many cities that were not on the envelope. This puzzled me. Could it be that the conductor forgot about me and I had missed Akron? The sun had set and it was getting dark. Soon it would be nighttime and still no sign of Akron or the conductor. I continued looking out the window. It was hard to read the names of the cities, but I did not want to fall asleep, just in case I would miss Akron. Some of the other passengers were sleeping. We did not speak each other's language so we could not communicate. During the night, the conductor stopped by with a colleague. I assumed he was trying to tell me that his shift was finished and his colleague would see me safely to Akron. It was reassuring to know that at least they had not forgotten about me. I resumed my task of watching the countryside. I had no idea how big, bigger than big, this country was.

I kept my vigil all night. It was daybreak and shortly the sun would rise. I was glued to the window, not missing anything along the way. Vast open spaces, forests, hills, mountains, and large and small cities, I wanted to take it all in. I was hungry, but then I was used to being hungry. I had no idea how much longer it would take. I gave up on that little map. It did not match the real world out there.

Once again the train stopped, as it had many times along the way, but this time the conductor came to my compartment and announced that we were in Akron. Several of the passengers were getting ready to depart. A "red cap" attendant helped them with their suitcases and packages. I noticed that people were giving them money for this service. I had a very small suitcase with only a few belongings. It did not even weigh five pounds. The "red cap" took my suitcase and motioned to follow him. I knew I had to pay this man but I did not know how much. I only had the $5.00, so I gave it to him. He smiled, bowed, and said something that I did not understand.

I stood on the platform of the railroad depot of Akron. There were several people waiting to meet the passengers. I wore a pair of black jeans with a faded old maroon sweatshirt. My nametag was tied to the zipper of the sweatshirt. People all around were dressed in warm coats. I felt shabby, so out of place. I was self-conscious about my appearance. I did not know if my relatives even knew I was coming. Of course, I had never met them so I did not know what they looked like. Startled, I heard someone calling my name. Hesitantly, I started walking toward the voice. Three people stood together. The elderly woman was calling out my name. Beside her stood a tall elderly man and another much shorter man accompanied them. I walked toward them. The woman stepped forward to meet me. She introduced herself as my Aunt Julianna and then her husband, Uncle

Michael. The gentleman with them was the treasurer of the Portage Country Club in Akron, a man whose name I cannot remember. He had driven my relatives to the train depot to pick me up. I sat in the backseat with my Aunt and started to cry, and could not stop. Why was I crying now? I seldom cried. Why now of all times? By the time we arrived home, I was in control of my emotions.

LIFE IN AMERICA

Aunt and Uncle lived in a cozy bungalow. Their living room was furnished with a comfortable sofa, armchairs, tables, several potted plants, Uncle Michael's favorite rocking chair, and a television. I had never seen a television before. They had their own bedrooms. The kitchen had modern appliances and conveniences. I just stared, amazed, *Wow*, escaped my lips. Their home was spotless and orderly.

Aunt Julianna had prepared a hot tub of bubble bath for me. I was luxuriating in the bubble bath while she took my clothing and deposited them in the basement. She gave me a bathrobe to use until proper clothing could be provided.

She had prepared a delicious dinner and I gratefully accepted everything she placed before me. It was during dinner that she had informed me how the relatives decided that I was to live with them. Uncle Steve and his wife did not want me to live with them in Louisville, Kentucky. Aunt Mary and her husband, they lived the next street over, did not want me either. In fact, I was not really wanted by any of my relatives living in the States. They had accepted the responsibility because Uncle Marton, their brother, had asked them to take good care of me. I just listened. It hurt very much to be unwanted by relatives who did not even know me and to be told so bluntly on the first day.

Uncle Michael, a relation by marriage to my aunt, was the only one determined to help me. Uncle Michael came to the States in early 1900. He met a young woman named Teresa. She was the sister of Uncle Marton. They married and moved to Akron. It was through the generosity of Uncle Michael that Teresa's sisters, Anna, with her husband, Mary, and her brother Steve, were able to immigrate to the States. He had provided for all of them until they found jobs, and he was not even a blood relative.

I was told that Uncle Michael adored his Teresa and that they had a happy life together. After the early death of Teresa, he was encouraged by the family to return to Hungary in 1948, to marry Teresa's sister, Julianna, whose husband had died during World War II, and then bring her to America. Uncle Michael and Teresa did not have any children and neither did Julianna and her late husband. Uncle Michael was getting up in years and needed a house-keeper and Julianna needed a home. The arrangement suited them both and they had a comfortable life together.

I soon learned that it was through the kindness and generosity of Uncle Michael that I came to live in their home. I knew I could never repay his kindness, but I was determined that I would do my best, so they would not regret helping me.

So many events took place on that first day. I was introduced to Aunt Mary and her husband and their three sons. I did not know I had cousins. The cousins were much older, married with homes of their own. It was a busy afternoon with people dropping in for a short visit. I felt I was on display.

I was very tired. So many things contributed to my weariness. The long airplane flight, the excitement of arrival, and the exhausting train trip. Emotionally, I was coping with my aunt's revelation of not being wanted by any of these people who came to see me. I was glad to be alone in the bedroom thinking of my parents and the loving home I had left behind. Quietly, I cried myself to sleep. Freedom had such a high price tag.

I saw that my elderly Uncle and Aunt had to make some adjustments in their daily routine to accommodate a teenager. I could have been their granddaughter. Aunt Julianna was an excellent cook and she knew the value of proper nutrition. She was determined that I would have proper nourishment and rest so I could get well. The atmosphere of their home was very formal and proper. As the days went by, I realized that they cared about my well-being even though they did not express it

Christmas of 1957 was approaching. Aunt Julianna announced that we were invited to Christmas dinner at the home of one of my cousins. She was cooking and baking in preparation for the dinner. I wondered, what would Christmas be like in America?

Christmas morning, after breakfast, Uncle Michael gave me a small box wrapped in shiny paper. It was so pretty, I just held it. After while I heard him say, "Open it." I opened it carefully, because I did not want to tear the pretty paper. He was watching me as I carefully lifted the lid of the box. Inside the box was a beautiful delicate gold watch. I looked at him with tears rolling down my face. I rose from my seat, walked over to him, wrapped my arms around his neck, and sobbed. He was a stately gentleman, and reminded me of my dear grandfather. He removed the watch from its case and fastened it to my wrist.

My relatives all lived close by. Cousin Alex and his wife Annie lived next door, so we rode with them across town to the "family" Christmas dinner. Cousin Bella and his wife Dorothy and their children lived in a huge sprawling ranch with a big yard. Their house was beautiful, the furniture, decorations, the spacious rooms, I had never seen anything like it. In the large living room, they had a floor to ceiling live Christmas tree with lights and all types of decorations. Packages of all sizes, wrapped in colorful paper were piled high under the tree. The women were busy in the kitchen. Aunt Mary told me to sit down in the living room until dinner was served. I found a chair in a corner and watched the activities unfold around me.

My mind wandered to a home far away, to a small room, where four people would be celebrating Christmas around a small tree, placed on the table, with homemade decorations. They would make sure that Frankie would get a much-needed article of clothing, maybe a shirt or socks. Mother and Father would exchange a homemade gift. Uncle Marton would be smoking his pipe, enjoying the company of his family. Oh, how I missed my beloved family. I sent them a letter shortly after I arrived in Akron, but I knew they would not receive it in time for Christmas. The call for dinner interrupted my remembrances.

This was more than a dinner. It was a feast to delight the senses. The table was laden with food. This was my first experience of being a guest in an American home. The abundance of material possessions was evident all around me. There was such luxury and an abundance of creature comforts I had never seen before. I could not imagine people living like that.

Following dinner, the family retired to the living room to open presents. Dorothy and Bella had two adorable small children. They were all excited, hovering around the Christmas tree, and could hardly wait to open their gifts. As package after package was opened, they revealed toys that would delight any child. The adults were exchanging gifts with delightful expressions of "ohs" and "ahs". As I gazed across the room, it reminded me of the store windows in New York City.

Later in my bed that night, my mind and heart were in a far away land, remembering a starlit night and holding my Father's hand as we walked home from the Christmas Eve service.

LIFE WITH RELATIVES

I spent the winter studying English. I wanted to help Aunt Julianna around the house but she was reluctant to accept my offer of help. I reassured her that I was capable of helping and knew how to work. She was old and I was confident that I was able to do whatever she needed. She finally accepted my offer of help under one condition, that I would do everything exactly as she told me. By now, I was very good at following instructions, since that is all I did most of my life. I felt like a robot. But if that was what it took for her to accept me, I was determined to do my very best to follow her instructions in all aspects of household duties such as cleaning house, helping with the laundry, ironing and washing dishes. She informed me that here in America we performed all these chores differently than in the old country. Yes, there were many more possessions and rooms to clean over here.

Aunt Julie, as I came to call her, was an excellent cook. I would stand by the stove and watch her prepare all the meals from scratch. I was ready and willing to help and learn if she would only let me. She wanted me to learn by watching her. I desired to learn by doing. All our meals were formal, from the linen tablecloths and napkins to the formal table setting. From the appetizer to the main course and the dessert, we ate our meals in silence. I was glad I was taught proper manners from early childhood. I noticed the approval in Aunt Julie's eyes the first time I had dinner with them. I was so eager to please them. I did not want them to regret ever taking me into their home.

Finally, the day came when Aunt Julie permitted me to start helping her in the kitchen. I truly do not believe that a surgeon had to scrub and clean any more than I did before I was allowed to help. I was taught the importance of cleanliness since I was a child and Aunt Julie was aware of that. I washed my hands in the bathroom, put on the apron, and tied the bandana over my hair. In the kitchen, she instructed me to scrub my hands up to my elbows at the kitchen sink with the unscented soap she kept there. After I finished scrubbing my hands, the second time, she handed me a fresh lemon slice to rub over my hands to remove any lingering soap residue. I felt she was overdoing it and my feelings were hurt. I obeyed her and learned a lot from her about the preparation of food, cooking and baking. Every time I helped her in the kitchen, I dutifully performed my "scrubbing" routine. I realized my obedience pleased her and she was willing to teach me. In time, I was able to help her with whatever she needed to do around the house.

In January of 1958, Uncle Michael arranged for a tutor to help me in learning the English language. I would see Mrs. Parsons Monday through Friday for the next six months. She was an excellent teacher and she prepared me to start school in September.

One afternoon, when I returned from English classes, I found Aunt Julie troubled by something. Uncle Michael asked her what was bothering her. She told him that the woman who did her toenails was not able to do it. Eagerly I volunteered, "Aunt Julie, I can cut your toenails."

"You, you know how to cut toenails?" she snapped.

"Yes, I cut my own," I replied.

"It's not the same," she said somewhat irritated.

I mused, what is the big deal about cutting toenails? Uncle Michael observed that we were not getting anywhere so he said, "Let her do it."

Later that evening, after her bath, she joined us in the living room. I was ready with towel, nail clippers, file, and lotion, waiting to cut her toenails. I told her she would be more comfortable if she reclined on the sofa and put her feet on the towel in my lap. I cut her toenails and finished with rubbing lotion on her feet. She thanked me and admitted I was very gentle. I said I would be happy to cut her toenails anytime. As time went on, she even let me set her hair every Saturday. I wanted to please them with all my heart. They were good people. In their old age, they had accepted a big responsibility to take care of me.

MEETING NEIGHBORS

Helen, a gracious young woman with an adorable little boy, was one of our neighbors. Helen's mother was a friend of Aunt Julie. Shortly after my arrival, Helen dropped by with several dresses, skirts, sweaters, and blouses—all gifts for me. I was a total stranger to this lovely young woman but over the next two years, she purchased many outfits for me. She took me shopping and helped me pick out clothing appropriate for a teenager. She introduced me to some of the American customs. We went to a drive-in and she treated me to a cheeseburger with all the fixings, fries, and coke, afterwards we went to a movie. Helen and her parents were generous people. There was laughter in their home. Their home had a relaxed and comfortable atmosphere. I had fun playing with little Harry. He was four years old and he was teaching me English. We laughed and rolled on the carpet, as he eagerly told me the name of everything around us, waiting for me to repeat it after him. Every Sunday afternoon during the summer, the family would go for a picnic and they always invited me.

FIRST JOB

Uncle Michael welcomed my presence in their home from the first day. I needed a home and he was able to provide one, and that settled it for him. It took a little longer for Aunt Julie to accept me. When she realized that I was eager to please her and help her, she began to warm towards me. Aunt Mary was something else. For some reason, she acted as if I was some sort of threat to her. She did not like me. She was unhappy that Uncle Michael and Aunt Julie had accepted me. It upset her very much that Uncle Michael was sending me to school. It was a source of argument between them. Uncle Michael told her it was none of her business. He was not going to send a sixteen-year-old to work. I needed to go to school. Aunt Mary would not give up. Every time she visited, she cornered me and scolded me saying I should be ashamed of myself living off my elderly relatives. If I had any decency, I would find a job. Once a week, she and Aunt Julie went grocery shopping together. After these outings, Aunt Julie would be reserved. Aunt

Mary would be hateful. It upset Uncle Michael; he did not want anyone to meddle in his home. I felt miserable.

Irene was a beautician, she owned her own salon, and both my aunts were her clients. Aunt Julie introduced us when I had my first haircut. Irene was an outgoing sociable businesswoman. I liked her and she took an interest in me. It was June of 1958, and Mrs. Parsons had finished tutoring me. She had also arranged for me to start classes at Kenmore High School in September. Irene had an idea; she asked my Aunt if I could help her during the summer. She had a large clientele and it would benefit both of us. She could use my help, and I would be exposed to English speaking people. Uncle Michael did not like the idea. He did not want me to work. Aunt Julie thought it would be good for me since she, herself, would not learn English. Aunt Mary was delighted. She let me know I was a burden and that I should start repaying my Uncle.

Monday through Friday I would walk to Irene's beauty shop to work for four hours. Irene's husband had died many years ago. She told some of her friends that I was her daughter, and I was studying in Europe, and had just returned for the summer. She treated me like her daughter. Each week she would style my hair differently. We shopped and she would buy me clothes. She owned a sporty convertible and she would invite me to her home, a beautiful old lakefront house with a large yard in the Portage Lakes. She confided to me that she had always wanted a daughter. Strangers liked me and accepted me. Why did Aunt Mary hate me? I could not understand it. Why was she always causing arguments and hard feelings between Aunt Julie and Uncle Michael? I felt they had a peaceful home until I came.

I received my first pay from Irene. She had done more for me than I did for her, yet she insisted that I take it. All the way home, I planned to give that money to Uncle Michael. After all, as Aunt Mary had made it abundantly clear it was about time.

Uncle Michael was sitting in his favorite rocker when I got home. We chatted a little, then I gave him the money. He was very upset with me. What was I thinking, repaying him? He was more than capable of providing for a young girl. How could I ever think that kindness should be repaid? He returned the money, marched into his room, and did not speak to me for the rest of the day. He was deeply offended that I even thought he was so mean spirited that he would want the money. I was devastated. We ate our dinner in silence. After we cleaned up the kitchen, I went outside and hid behind the pine trees in the backyard. I was broken hearted that I had offended my Uncle. I could not explain; he was so offended, he would not listen to me.

I did what Aunt Mary wanted me to do, I did it willingly, was happy to do it. What did I do wrong? I was afraid to return to the house. It was getting dark and no one came to look for me. Tears were rolling down my face. Uncle Michael was in his room when I timidly walked in. Aunt Julie declared that I had offended him and that I should be ashamed of myself, and that was not the way to repay his kindness. I could not defend myself; it was no use trying to tell her that I had no desire to offend them.

LEARNING ABOUT PREJUDICE

The following week Irene needed help. She talked with Aunt Julie if I could stay with her for the entire day. When I arrived at work, she asked me to spend several days at her home on the lake while she had some drainage repair done on her property. The owner of the business would pick me up and bring me back each day. I was glad to help her out and I liked her home. It was beautiful there with several large shade trees covering the lawn, and it was quiet and peaceful by the lake.

I was in her office when she called for me, my ride was here. In the waiting room stood a very tall black man. He was dressed in a pair of jeans and a white T-shirt. I guessed his age, late thirties or early forties. He was the second person of his race I met since the young man in New York City. I smiled as we walked out to his car. He sat in the driver's seat, reached over to the passenger side, and opened the door. I sat down, turned slightly so I could face him. He did not say a word. He had both hands on the wheel and looked straight ahead. I felt he was very uncomfortable. I did not know anything about cars. Uncle Michael was too old to drive. Aunt Mary drove a car with the name of Buick on it. Our neighbor Helen also had a Buick. Since I made him very uncomfortable, I glanced around the interior of his car. It was a big car, the outside was white, and the interior was black leather. I had heard about the Cadillac, but never had seen one before. I was trying to figure out why he would not talk to me. Maybe he did not want me to ride in his car. I was dressed appropriately; he did not have to be ashamed to be seen with me. It was a long drive to the lake and every time we came to a stop sign or a traffic light, people would be screaming something at him that made the muscles on his arms and face flex and tighten. I did not understand what was happening. I arrived only six months ago and spent most of my time at home studying. I knew very little of the realities of the outside world.

Finally, he glanced at me and asked, "Are you prejudiced?" I did not know that word. The dictionary was in my bag, but I was not sure how to spell it. I realized he was waiting for my response. He did not know I could not speak English. He assumed I was Irene's daughter. Guessing, I answered him, "No, I am Catholic." At that, he burst out in a sarcastic laugh and said something. I was trying to piece together his words and realized he did not ask what religion I professed. He glanced at me again, "Don't you know what prejudice means?" I shook my head. "It means that white men don't want to see a white girl with a black man." Now I understood his discomfort, it was not my presence in his car; it was society's rejection of it, which made him uncomfortable. Feeling awkward, I responded, "That's a problem. Do you want me to walk?" He snorted, and was silent the rest of the way. I wanted to slide down in the seat so no one could see me. I felt so awful.

I was relieved when we arrived at Irene's home. He reached across to open the door. Waiting for him were two of his men with trucks and equipment, ready to work. He joined his men and I unlocked the house and went inside. I walked from room to room, opening windows when I over heard him telling the men what transpired along the way. The men laughed, but he was concerned about this spoiled girl who could get him in trouble. I wished I could reassure him that I was not spoiled and would not get him in trouble whatever he meant by that.

They started work around the foundation of the house, digging deep trenches, and repairing the drain. Irene's kitchen needed cleaning, and that kept me busy. Time went by so fast, when I noticed the men were sitting under one of the shade trees having lunch. I grabbed the dictionary and headed out to inquire if they needed anything. Wondering why I was there, all three stood up and waited to see what I wanted. One of the men was older than my "chauffeur" and the other one was a young man. I walked up to them and extended my hand to the older man and introduced myself. I shook hands with the young man. I explained to them I was new to this country and could not speak their language but I had a dictionary and we could communicate. I sat down on the ground, and waited for them to sit down. They must have figured since she was not going to go away, might as well join her.

The older man asked the first question. He remembered seeing pictures on the news about our freedom fight. He expressed his disappointment that America did not come to our aid. The young man wanted to know how I escaped. We shared bits and pieces about our lives and families. My "chauffeur" did not join our conversation; he just watched and listened.

Riding back to the beauty shop was a repeat of our morning drive. I still felt so awful, he was doing a favor for Irene, and yet he was condemned for doing it.

He was waiting for me the following morning. I understood why he would think that I was spoiled. I had lovely clothes; I looked like a typical American teenager. Yet I was atypical, a product of another culture. I was raised to respect all people. I felt comfortable talking with others, and I enjoyed learning more about them. I really wanted to know if what we learned about the Negro in school was true or just communist propaganda. During our morning drive, we talked very little. I could not understand the jeers of those idiots along the road. I could not fathom grown men being so cruel. I hated the ride, and I was glad when we arrived at the lake. The men started to work and I continued my house cleaning. Again, I did not notice it was lunchtime until I heard a voice at the kitchen window calling, "Miss Charlotte, are you going to join us?" It was my "chauffeur." I grabbed my dictionary and joined them. I tried to explain how his calling me was similar to what we did as children, visiting a friend's house to ask if they could come out and play. The men laughed so hard the youngest one was rolling in the grass. I was so pleased that they felt comfortable around me. I told them about picking cotton. They told me about slavery. We talked about their families. The young man was the son of the older man. My "chauffeur" watched and listened. At the end of the day, he would call, "Miss Charlotte, your chauffeur is waiting." I was looking forward to the next day. I enjoyed watching them work, listening to them talk and sharing their company.

The third day at lunch time, he poked his head through the kitchen window and called,"Little girl, can you come out and play?" I knew he was teasing, remembering my comment from yesterday. We would spend lunchtime under the shade tree and I learned about the men and their families. It was refreshing to hear how they paid attention to what was happening around the world. They were aware of current events and even those outside the United States. I have met Americans who did not know where Hungary was located. Some even asked if we lived in houses. I was tempted to say, no, in caves.

Sadly, at the end of the week, I knew their work was done. They were grading the soil around the house. I was going to miss them. They accepted me, a sixteen-year-old, as their equal. It was time to say good-bye. The older man took my hand in both of his and asked God to bless me. The young man wished me good luck with my studies. I turned to my "chauffeur", holding out my hand, instead of shaking my hand, he reached and hugged me. I put both of my arms around his neck and hugged him back. I believe it surprised him, for he quickly dropped his hands. I looked up into his face and smiled. I heard the older man say, "I told you she doesn't have a prejudice bone in her body." There was that word again. I meant to look it up.

The men were loading their equipment in the truck, ready to leave. I locked up the house. For the the last time I heard, "Miss Charlotte, your chauffeur is waiting." As soon as I sat down, I reached for the dictionary. Watching me, he asked, "What are you looking for?"

"Prejudice bone," I replied.

With a smile in his eyes, he teased, "It means, you are a Catholic."

Even though we encountered the jeers of some men, it did not matter. I had spent a week in a company of three kind men, real men, who understood suffering, and bore it with dignity. For the last time he reached across to open the door. As I stepped out he also stepped out of his car and standing tall said, "Good-bye little girl."

I learned a bittersweet lesson that week. America, the birthplace of freedom, denied basic rights to her own people. I was shocked and disappointed as I realized man's inhumanity to man was also very evident in the land of the free and the brave. The memory of our freedom fight was all too fresh. Freedom is so precious; people give their lives for it. If people would just sit down with a "dictionary" and pass it around, they would learn that we are all very much alike with hopes, dreams, and aspirations for ourselves, and for our families. What makes America great is our combined differences.

FAMILY VISITS

Uncle Steve traveled from Louisville, Kentucky, to visit us that summer. While I was in Hungary, Uncle Marton shared some background information about him. As a young man, he left Hungary and lived in Austria, Germany, France, Italy, Holland, and England for several years before coming to the States. He spoke several languages. I was looking forward to meeting him. Aunt Julie loved her brother, she was very happy to see him.

It did not take long before Uncle Steve reminded me that I should be very grateful for Uncle Michael and Aunt Julie taking me in. When he heard, Uncle Michael reminded him how he too needed a home for several months before he decided to move to Kentucky. I understood that Uncle Michael, with his formal and stern demeanor, had a kind and gentle heart. He had compassion for this young girl, who so wanted to be accepted and loved.

SCHOOL IN AMERICA

In September of 1958, I started high school. I was the object of curiosity and the center of attention for several weeks, until my classmates got used to me. I could not believe it when the dean asked which subjects I wanted to take. It did not matter which subjects I chose, I was here to study English. The teaching style was very relaxed, so different from that in Hungary. I liked my teachers. It was unusual to go from classroom to classroom. We had study hall and the classes lasted all day.

It upset Aunt Mary very much that I dared to go to school. She had no control over Uncle Michael, but Aunt Julie was afraid of her. She depended on her sister to take her to the store and any other appointments and Aunt Mary had a nasty temper. Aunt Mary always chose to visit when Uncle Michael was at work. She complained, again, that I should be working instead of going to school. She accused me of taking advantage of my relatives, and was certain I probably had evil motives to inherit their money. All this time, Aunt Mary had not given me one dollar, not even a penny, and my being here did not cost her one cent, nor deprived her of anything. Yet she was obsessed with the money my Uncle spent on my keep. Why? She had a comfortable home, car, and all the creature comforts she desired. Why was she lashing out at a defenseless young girl? I had not done anything to offend her. I did not want anything from her.

During one visit, she became furious, her face red with anger, verbally attacking me. She claimed, "We had no reason to start a revolution in Hungary. We should have been satisfied with our communist government; it was improving our lives, and we just did not realize how good we had it." For the first time since I came here, I had enough. I looked her straight in the eye and in a cold flat tone stated, "If you think that communism is so wonderful, why don't you pack your suitcase and move back there. It is easy to talk about something you do not know anything about. It is easy to spout your foul dogma in the country that guarantees you free speech, because as soon as you stepped across that border these freedoms would be denied to you. You live in such comfort and luxury that people over there cannot even imagine, let alone enjoy. You are a stinking communist. I never wanted anything from you. I did not even know you existed. It was Uncle Michael who opened his home to me and I am grateful to him, more than you'll ever know." Escaping her poison, I went into the bedroom and closed the door. I heard her say something nasty to Aunt Julie, warning her that she was not safe with me in her home.

THANKING GOD FOR HIS BLESSING

Ever since I landed in America, I wanted to thank God for His goodness in bringing me to this free country. This land blessed with freedom, opportunity, and an abundance of material possessions. My relatives did not attend church. Where could I go to thank God? They explained the many denominations and churches. I did not know anything about denominations. From my brief early childhood experience in Hungary, I knew a little about the Catholic Church. One was located a few blocks away. Since I walked to school, to Irene's, I was used to walking, and I did not mind walking to that church. It reminded me of the ones in Hungary. There were statues and paintings, various altars and the hushed silence as people made their way to the pews, it was all very familiar. I was hoping to recapture the same feelings I had when our little church opened its door for the first time in Kislang. It did not happen. I knew God lived in this building, and it was here I should to express my gratitude, to thank Him for guiding me and keeping me safe. I said all the prayers I could think of expressing the feelings of my heart. I settled in the pew and listened as the service started. It was the same as I remembered. We stood up, knelt down, said prayers, and sang hymns I did not know. The priest read from the Bible in Latin. I did not understand it in Hungary and I did not understand it here. It was all so hollow and empty.

Up to this time, people in my life in America never talked about God or attended church. I assumed people did not need God in this land of plenty and prosperity. Why did I feel empty, incomplete? Wanting to know God, an ever-present longing, filled my entire being. Ever since religion classes were banned and the church doors closed, I was troubled by the sin question. I knew I did not commit any of the cardinal sins, but I sinned. I knew, without a doubt, there was a God and I would be accountable to Him.

Aunt Julie was a pious woman. She prayed every day. At the same time, she was extremely superstitious. I could not fathom how in this day and age, anyone could be superstitious. On New Year's Eve at the stroke of midnight, she would walk down the steps to the basement alone. Over a candle she would melt lead in a special tablespoon and carefully pour the molten lead into a bowl of cold water. The molten lead when poured into cold water created a weird shaped object. She carefully studied the shape, and then held it up against the wall with the candle light casting a shadow over it. The form of the object and the shadows on the wall would foretell events for the coming year. She would perform this ritual for all the family members but for others she poured the lead with her left hand. She had placed a crucifix, holy water, and other objects inside and outside the house to keep evil spirits out. She would recite some kind of incantation against bad luck.

Uncle Michael believed in God. He felt he was a good man who helped many people. He was honest in his dealings with his fellowman thus his good deeds would outweigh the bad ones. He had no use for the church. Some of the people he knew, who always attended church, were not nice. Obviously, attending church did not do anything for them.

Aunt Mary and her husband were atheists. They were communist sympathizers and as far as they were concerned, God did not exist.

Cousin Alex, Aunt Mary's oldest son, and his wife Annie lived next door. Alex was a talented violinist. Alex was quite unlike his mother; he was kind and many times he encouraged me when his mother was cruel to me. Annie was an avid reader and she owned many books. On some evenings, I would cross the yard to visit. They had a comfortable and welcoming home. Alex liked to tease. Annie was always willing to help me with English and the proper pronunciation of words. They were high school sweethearts when they married and it was evident they loved each other very much.

I could talk to Annie about everything. She was a good listener. I noticed that many of the books in her library were about religions, mysticism, the occult, and spiritualism. Seeing those books aroused my curiosity to ask questions about them. We talked about Catholicism since I was most familiar with that one. I soon learned she was very knowledgeable about many of the world religions. She spent most of her adult life reading about Buddhism, Hinduism, she believed in reincarnation, she read the works of Confucius and she studied many of the Eastern religions. She practiced the occult, attended séances to communicate with the dead, read the Tarot cards, and regularly visited a reader and advisor. She had five spirit guides who would communicate with her. Over the next two years, I read many of her books and listened to her stories.

She believed that all religions led to God, and we had spirit guides to take us there. She was a night person and would be up most of the night and sleep during the day. It was during the night, while meditating, that these spirit guides would come to her. During my visit one evening she revealed to me that her spirit guides were accepting my presence. She introduced: a lama from Tibet, her main mentor; an Egyptian slave girl; Blue Feather, an American Indian; and a teacher from India. The teacher from India communicated with her via a pencil and notebook she kept by her chair. The pencil, without anyone holding it, would write a message to her. One of these messages informed her, at a certain point in time, this mentor would materialize for her to see. She confessed one night she saw bare feet and part of the legs, not quite to the knees, standing by her chair. I shivered; now that was getting to be creepy!

As she prayed and meditated in her office, she was surrounded by a variety of ancient artifacts, a crucifix, a Bible, Hindu prayer books and beads, holy water, scarab beetles, and eagle feathers. With incense burning, she would pray and chant and her spirit guides would lead her.

Her spirit guides might have accepted my presence, but I did not believe in them. I did not meditate or pray to them, all of it seemed so much hocus-pocus. Months went by, and occasionally, we would talk about these things. I read many of her books and wrote notes in my journal. One evening when I returned her book, I heard Alex playing his violin in the bedroom. The atmosphere of their home was peaceful as Annie and I listened and relaxed in their living room. Then strange things began to happen. Books, in her built in bookcase, were moving on the shelves. She greeted the teacher from India. Then a loud snapping noise, like wood splitting, sounded from a corner of the room. She greeted Blue Feather. She looked at me and said, "Don't be afraid, turn around slowly, there are two blue lights over your head." I did. Sure enough, there were two beautiful glowing blue lights over my head. Annie was very pleased. Her spirit guides appeared while I was visiting. She said they only come when it is peaceful, with no evidence of strife or tension in the room. I was not afraid, yet I did not like the feeling that washed over me. I had the ominous feeling of being in the presence of something ancient and old from another world, the world of the dead. Anne talked about the world of the unseen spirits and the warfare between the good and evil spirits.

For Christmas in 1959, Annie gave me a beautiful, fourteen-carat antique gold necklace with a cluster of jade grapes in the center. The Indian teacher spirit guide told her where to find the necklace. This Indian teacher would protect and lead me when I was ready. In the meantime, I was to wear it at all times. I wore the necklace because it was beautiful. For good luck, she gave me a Bible. I did not regard the Bible as a good luck charm. It was a precious book; Grandmother believed it contained the Word of God. I remembered when the communists invaded, confiscating all the Bibles and burning them. I never saw a

Bible before. Yes, there was the big Bible on the altar in our church but only the priest could read it. Wonder of wonders, I held a Bible in my hands. Carefully I ran my fingers over its cover, which read HOLY BIBLE. It was an authorized King James Version.

I could hardly wait to start reading it. As with all books, one starts in the beginning. In Genesis, I found many of the stories the priest taught us in religion classes. It was wonderful to read but I had difficulty finding some of the words in the dictionary. I had no problem with Thee and Thou, after all, no one could call God, You, it would be disrespectful.

Exodus was exciting, because it resonated with my spirit of justice being served to the evil doers. Such adventures, God was leading His people out of Egypt, and protecting them from the cruel taskmasters. All those plagues and miracles He performed on their behalf. What a God! The Ten Commandments were here too. We memorized them when we studied about sin in religion class. However, it was slow reading. My vocabulary was limited and there were many words I could not understand. I was a biblical illiterate; I did not know anything about the Bible. I reasoned it was so difficult to understand, and had words I could not pronounce, because, as the cover said, it was a Holy Bible, and it probably was a holy language.

I made it to Leviticus. It was a book full of laws and rituals, and I could not understand the altars, burnt sacrifices, and bullocks. What was a bullock? Clean and unclean animals, peace offerings, sin offerings, killing animals and sprinkling blood, I could not comprehend that people actually did that. Where would I have to go to do all those things? Trying to read it, let alone make sense of it, was hard. I could not even remember all those things, let alone do them. I could barely remember the admonitions we were taught in religion class, how could I remember all these new things? As students, we were always directed to do this and to do that. As a small child, I could not even understand them, let alone obey them. Maybe the saints, whose pictures and statues adorned the walls of churches and cathedrals, and who suffered martyrdom for their faith, were able to do all these things. As for me, God remained inaccessible.

I had spent two years studying eastern religions. They all had one thing in common, man's attempt to earn his way into God's grace by good works. The Catholics had hosts of saints to intercede for them. The Buddhists and Hindus had hundreds of idols to pray to, spirit worship and spirit guides to lead the faithful. I unclasped the gold necklace; I did not want any spirit to lead me. I was in turmoil. I had far more questions than solid answers. How would I know what kind of good works pleased God? How many and how often would I have to do them? Why do we all hope for our good deeds to outweigh our bad ones? Why do we hope, that somehow, the scales would tip in our favor and we could say, look at me, God, I am good, I did all these great deeds for you. On the other hand, if we messed up in this life maybe in the next reincarnation, we could do better.

I just knew there has to be more, more to life than frustration and searching for answers. Deep inside all of us is a seed of consciousness, knowing that we are held accountable to a Higher Power. There will come a day when we have to give an account. We have a desire within to demand justice. We want evil doers to be punished, such as the Hitlers and Stalins and all those who committed atrocities against mankind. We like to compare ourselves to others; after all, we are not as bad as so and so. With over two years of searching and studying, I concluded that religions are frustrating, impossible to keep, and if they made one so miserable, who needs it. If it were even possible to know God, He would have to reveal it to me.

CHANGES BEYOND MY CONTROL

I was eighteen and the summer of 1960 brought many changes into my life. Aunt Mary was relentless in her goal of evicting me from my Uncle's home. She demanded that I work. She made sure I would, since she found a job at a diner in downtown Akron, where I could take the bus back and forth to work. The owner was a Greek and he employed two Greek women. All of them were kind to me. The women showed me how to wait on tables. Even the cooks were helpful when I tried to place the orders for the customers.

I started early morning and it was late afternoon by the time I returned home. I began noticing changes in Aunt Julie. I did not understand what was happening or why. She was angry; it was unlike her. She would throw dishes in the sink and slam doors. She said horrible things, hurtful things, like why did she ever take this evil person into her home. Uncle Michael was distressed; his peaceful home was destroyed, and Aunt Julie would not even speak to him. She refused any offer of help around the house and ordered me to get out of her sight. I turned to Uncle Michael for advice. What was I to do? I could not ignore the situation, and I could not let him live like this in his old age. I decided as soon as I found a place, I would move out. He was very much against it, did not even want to hear about it. I was determined to move as soon as possible.

I asked the Greek women if they knew of a room for rent. I earned $35.00 a month at the restaurant, and I had saved $20.00 while I worked for Irene. I could get by on that. A week later, one of the Greek women invited me to her home. Her neighbor, Linda, an elderly widow, lived across the street in a large house. She rented two rooms, one to an elderly woman, and she might be interested in renting the other room to me. I met with Linda and we talked about the possibility of renting from her. She hesitated, she had to think about renting to a young girl. After Linda left, I felt dejected. I was getting ready to walk home when the doorbell rang. It was Linda, and she had changed her mind and wanted me to see the room. We walked across the street. She had a big two-story house and the bedrooms were upstairs. Her renter had the two rooms facing the street. At the top of the stairs was a smaller bedroom with a double bed, dresser, chest of drawers, cedar chest, a sewing machine and a small closet. Linda offered to clean out the closet and dresser and I could have the room for $7.00

a week. This was my opportunity, and I said I would take it. At my words, she impulsively hugged me.

From Linda's place, I walked slowly home. I needed time to think how I would break the news to Uncle Michael. I tried to tell him gently, I told him about the two old women and the room I could rent, how it was still in Kenmore and not that far. I had a job for the summer and I would return to school in the fall to finish the last year. He was hurt. He never wanted me to leave under such circumstances. Nevertheless, there was something terribly wrong with Aunt Julie. She was angry, with outbursts of violence, her emotions were out of control, and it was so unlike her. I hoped their life would return to normal, after I left.

The next morning, I packed my clothes and books. All my possessions fit in a small suitcase, two boxes, and four shopping bags. I called a cab. Since Uncle Michael was working, it made it so much easier to leave. Aunt Julie never came out of the kitchen where she was slamming cupboard doors and throwing things. I set the house keys on the dresser, left my room neat and tidy, and then I carried my belongings outside and waited for the cab.

The cab driver pulled in the driveway, took one look at the packages, and grumbled, "His was a cab and not a moving truck." I had no other way of moving my few belongings. I gave him the address, and then he became downright nasty. I was fighting back the tears, and I could hardly wait to get out of his cab. If that was how he treated all his customers, I wondered why he still had a job. I was relieved when he stopped in front of Linda's house. He pointed to the meter, indicating that I owed him $1.89. I reached in my purse and pulled out a $10.00 bill and gave it to him, got out of the cab and started to take out my things. All of a sudden, this nasty man was falling over himself, "May I help you with the packages, miss?" Quietly, I responded, "No, thank you."

Watching for me at her window, Linda, in her seventies, ran out to welcome me. She picked up some of the bags and led the way into the house. I unpacked the dresses and hung them in the closet to make room for the rest of the bags. I ran up and down the stairs discarding the boxes and bags. Rather quickly, the room was in order. Finally, I sat down the edge of the bed and looked around.

It was a tiny room. The double bed was in a corner of the room, against the wall. At the end of the bed was the dresser. To the left of the bed was a small closet, the door would only open half way because the chest of drawers blocked the opening. Beside the chest of drawers was the cedar chest next the bedroom door. On the other side of the door was a sewing machine next to the window. As I looked around, I realized I had approximately two feet of space at the side and the foot of my bed to move around. The room was used to store furniture that did not fit anywhere else in the house.

I opened the window to let in fresh air. I turned and noticed a small picture of Franklin Delano Roosevelt over the bed. There was another picture over the cedar chest; I thought it looked like a photograph. I walked over to take a closer look, I could not figure out what it was. Then I recognized it. I had to place my hands over my mouth to stifle a scream. It was a photo of a dead body lying in a casket. My thoughts reeled, how bizarre, why would anyone take a picture of a dead body in a casket, frame it, and hang it on a wall? Wouldn't people rather remember their loved one alive, instead of this, this, corpse? I was trembling. This was Death. I wanted to flee. I was trapped in a room with Death. Shaking, I turned the light off and climbed into bed, pulling the covers up to my chin. By now, it was nighttime and I could not see the picture with the light off, but even with my eyes closed, I could see that dead body in the casket. I lay in bed and cried; I felt all alone.

First thing in the morning, I searched for a postcard to cover that casket. With trembling hands, I pushed the postcard between the frame and the glass. It did not cover the entire picture, but at least it hid the upper part of the body. When she sent that card, I am sure my girlfriend did not realize just what use I would find for it.

ALONE

I was all alone. I had no friends. All the people I knew were old enough to be my grandparents or my parents. When I left my Uncle's home, I left all those friends and neighbors behind. I had no friends my own age since Aunt Mary warned me I was not to make friends with anyone in school and never to invite anyone home. My life consisted of going to school, working around the house and studying. I had no social life. I wrote letters to my parents and my friends in Hungary. I received a Hungarian/English dictionary in New York City and I spent time memorizing it. I wanted to build my vocabulary so I could communicate better.

I rode the bus to work in the morning and at the end of the shift, Aspasia's husband would pick us both up. As the days passed, I discovered that our Greek neighbors were very social and entertained often. I would help Aspasia to polish the silver and her beautiful table settings for these events. Linda had many friends and belonged to several clubs so she would be away most of the day. Her house desperately needed cleaning. On Saturday mornings, I would clean my room and our shared bathroom. One day, as usual, I was all alone in the house, so I decided to clean the entire house. I scrubbed, mopped, and dusted all the rooms downstairs until everything was spotless clean and shining. I was upstairs in my room reading when Linda returned home. Next thing I knew, she was in my room hugging me, and thanking me for cleaning her house. We made a deal; she would do my laundry and ironing once a week and fix my breakfast every morning in exchange for cleaning her house. She said, "One kind deed deserved another." She knew I had no means of washing my clothes and no place to store food.

I had to budget my money carefully. I earned $35.00 a month and I paid $28.00 a month for rent, with $7.00 left for personal items. Occasionally, I could eat something at the diner but the owner was not handing out free meals. For breakfast, I ate toast and coffee with Linda and a glass of juice. When I worked with Aspasia, she always saved a piece of pie for us to eat at the end of our shift.

September 1960 was rapidly approaching. I informed the owner of the diner that I could not work my regular shift, because I would be starting school. If he needed help after school, I would be happy to work because I needed a job. He snapped, "You're a girl, and you don't need an education." He said that to the wrong person. I retorted, "That

is your opinion, Sir, and I don't happen to agree with you."
He never gave me a final answer so the following Monday
I did not show up to work, I started school instead.

Without a job, I would soon be desperate. I had my
$20.00 savings and the few dollars left over from rent. I
agonized, what was I going to do? I must find another job,
I must be able to support myself. Linda, bless her, asked all
her friends, if anyone heard of a job opening. I knew I was
not very marketable, I had no skills, and I was still in school.
Long worrisome days dragged by as I hoped and waited for
a job. Dear Linda was not just my landlady; she was a real
friend. While I was in school, she was job hunting on my
behalf and one day she had good news. A friend of hers,
Mrs. Kelly, owned a small diner on Kenmore Boulevard,
a couple of blocks from our house. Because her employee
was moving, Mrs. Kelly needed someone part time from
2:00 p.m. to 7:00 p.m., Monday to Friday, and a half a day
on Saturdays. Linda praised me, so Mrs. Kelly wanted to
meet me. She would pay $10.00 a week. I was so relieved
and very delighted.

Mrs. Kelly and her husband were in their late sixties. A
jovial and kind couple, they worked as a team in their business. She did the cooking and he did the dishes and cleaning. Mrs. Kelly graciously showed me what she expected
of me as her employee. After the first week of orientation,

she left me to run the place while she made afternoon visits to her friends. As expected, the busiest times in the diner were in the morning for the breakfast crowd, then lunchtime, and evenings. The hours between 2:00 p.m. and 4:30 p.m. were very quiet. To keep busy, I would wash down the shelves, cupboards, and windows, anything that needed a touch of freshening. Many afternoons I would help Mr. Kelly do the dishes. This made him happy, he could have a little time to rest and read the paper before the evening rush. I would defrost the refrigerator and clean the grill, the soda fountain, the things that Mrs. Kelly always did. I must admit it made me feel good to know she appreciated my efforts. She would tell her friends and customers what a good worker her new helper was.

I did not realize it at the time, but God was at work in my life arranging circumstances, bringing people into my life to come along and help me, encouraging me at the very time when I was at the end of my resources.

My days passed going to school, working at the diner, and studying in the evenings. I spent hours and hours memorizing my dictionary, building my vocabulary so it would be easier for me to understand what I was reading and studying. It was tiresome to open the dictionary at every other word to find out its meaning. I would sit by the window and study late into the night. I placed the Holy

Bible on the dresser and I would notice it lying there but I was afraid to read it. I knew deep in my heart I could never learn or keep all those rules in Leviticus. The Bible was a reminder that I could never please God if I could not even remember those laws.

As a small child, I remembered hearing Grandmother and her friend talking about the Bible and how within its pages were written events that would take place in the future. It all sounded so strange and mysterious. Now, as I gazed at the Bible, I wondered where in all those pages it could be. I always was an avid reader. I especially loved to read adventures and mysteries, many times I could not wait to find out how the story would end, so I would read the last chapter to find out. Not knowing any differently, I assumed the Bible must be the same way. Maybe, just maybe, if I would read the last chapter I could find out how it all ends. Looking in the table of contents, I turned the pages to the chapter called Revelation. Dictionary near by, I began reading. It started with messages to several churches. I puzzled what that meant. As I continued reading, I discovered I understood less and less. I had to search my dictionary for the words describing God's throne with all those creatures around it; everything about it seemed horrifying. Then there were the horses, a white, a red, a black, and a pale horse. Death sat on the pale horse. A cold chill ran through me. Unbelievable catastrophes happened all over the world. The Beast and some horrible creatures came out of the sea. All kinds of devastating events and disasters took place. I spent many hours way into the night searching my dictionary for the meaning of the words I could not understand.

The last book in the Bible was far more terrifying than Leviticus. Only the very last part of this book described a place of peace and beauty, a place where Jesus lived in the beautiful city, and all those who belonged to Him would live there forever. It upset me very much; I had no hope of ever living in that beautiful city. I was not good enough to go there. I was destined for purgatory.

GOD PROVIDES

It was obvious that Mrs. Kelly and her husband were fond of me. One evening as we were closing up, she declared I was too skinny and needed to eat regular meals. She insisted, "From now on I want to see you here every morning, before school, for breakfast." I walked home that evening with a grateful heart. I did not have enough money for toiletries let alone food. The next morning, I sat down with Mr. Kelly while Mrs. Kelly prepared our breakfast. She started with fresh grapefruit sections, followed by four pancakes, with sausage and eggs on the side, and a tall glass of milk. I stared at Mr. Kelly's plate, he had the same portions, but he was a big man. Gazing back at me with a twinkle in his eye, he said, "You better start eating."

I protested, "Mr. Kelly, I am not a farmhand, I cannot eat all this food."

"You better start, or you'll be late for school, and she won't let you leave until you clean your plate," he warned.

I pleaded, "I cannot eat all this." He smiled and moved his plate closer so I could transfer some of my food to his plate. Gratefully, I smiled back at him. He understood I could not possibly eat all that food, but his dear wife wanted to "fatten" me up and she persisted in serving farmhand portions. It became our morning ritual, he would move his plate closer so I could transfer portions of my food onto his plate, and then we would eat.

After school, she had lunch waiting, and at the end of the day, she served dinner. She would pack a cookie or a donut and a carton of milk so I could have a snack while studying. I came to love them and I willingly helped them beyond what they hired me to do.

The more I helped them, the more generous they became. It was mind-boggling. I was among strangers, yet they loved me and cared about me. Mrs. Kelly always ordered clothes from the department stores and had it delivered to the diner. One afternoon when I reported for work, she announced, "Let's go back to the staff lounge, I want to show you something." It was a classic little black dress with a short jacket. Assuming she wanted my opinion, I was happy to tell her, "It's stunning and you would look great in it."

She urged me to look closer, "I am sure it would not fit me." We stood side by side admiring the beautiful dress. "Look at the size, do I look like a size six?" she was smiling ear to ear, "it's yours." No, Mrs. Kelly was not a size six. She was a big woman with a kind heart as big as her body. "Try it on, model it for us," she asked, and she left so I could change. The dress was a perfect fit. It was the first of many gifts she gave to me while I worked for her.

Linda was more concerned about my lack of a social life than I was. Every evening she would wait for me to come home from work. I would stop and talk with her before going to my room to study and read. She would fuss that I was almost nineteen years old and all I did was work and study, day after day. "You need friends your age," she would say.

I smiled, and told her, "For the time being that was the way it had to be."

In my room, I would reflect on her comments and smile ruefully. I needed a whole lot more than friends my own age; I needed to find a job that would pay more than $10.00 a week. I could not go on living under these circumstances indefinitely. I pushed myself day after day to improve my vocabulary and language skills. I would have liked to go to college, but I felt it was an impossible dream. So many adults thought girls did not need higher education; instead, girls should marry and become homemakers. Even in school, I noticed that very few girls aspired to go to college. The uncertainty of my future weighed heavy upon me.

SEARCHING FOR GOD

I kept the Bible on the dresser and found myself drawn to it. I remembered when Annie gave me the Bible as a "good luck charm" to keep me from harm, she shared when they built their house she had a copy of Psalm 91 built into the foundation. I decided to find Psalm 91 in the Bible. I read it repeatedly and then I started reading the other Psalms; they were wonderful. The Psalms were easy to understand, and they spoke to my heart. They were not scary or terrifying or a list of impossible rules. I identified with them. Psalm 32 and Psalm 51 deeply touched my heart, tears would roll down my face onto the pages as I sat by the window and read. Whoever was this David, I could identify with him. David talked to his God, and he loved his God, in Psalm 32 he wrote that "Blessed is he whose transgression is forgiven, whose sin is covered." I marveled, how did that happen?

I had this longing, deep within my heart, to know, how are those sins covered and forgiven? I wondered if other people had similar feelings, or was I overly sensitive to these things.

INVITATION

Linda was all excited. Her family reunion was coming up and she had been talking about it for days. Frequently she made calls to her relative named Maggie. It appeared that they were conspiring about something. They had a large extended family of brothers, sisters, aunts, uncles, cousins, and relatives of all kinds and a guest would always be welcome. Daily, Linda would invite me. I was hesitant to accept her invitation. I enjoyed quiet days alone, actually, it was a welcomed change from studying and working all the time. Linda persisted, "Why would you want to sit in your room, all cooped up, when you could be having fun?" I preferred staying at home, but I accepted her invitation, since I did not want to hurt her feelings.

They held their family reunion out in the country at a large picnic ground with shelters. My, did they have relatives! Those attending numbered over a hundred, but there were some who could not come. During the day, Linda introduced me to most of her relatives. Just in case she missed anyone, before dinner when all the invited guests were introduced, she did the honors again. She and Maggie sat at the same table.

After dinner, as people started to mingle, Linda introduced me to the young man, Louis, sitting next to Maggie. Now I knew the reason for her insistence, it was so obvious; they had planned this meeting for days.

A week or so later, I received an invitation for dinner, followed by an invitation to visit his church. He said he was a Christian and he regularly attended church. I was not impressed, so what, did he think I was a heathen? I was not receptive to religions of any kind. I knew they were nothing more than a bunch of rules that no one could keep.

At the suggestion of Maggie, his landlady, he invited me to the Haven of Rest Rescue Mission for a Saturday evening service. I declined. Whoever heard of going to a place called Haven of Rest Rescue Mission on a date. What was that place? I consulted my dictionary and I tried to analyze it, Haven of Rest sounded nice and peaceful, somewhat tranquil. Rescue Mission, on the other hand, it had an ominous sound; besides, I did not need to be rescued from anything.

He persisted, extending the invitation, so, out of curiosity, I reluctantly accepted.

Free
at
Last

PART 5

HAVEN OF REST

Despite my dictionary, I still had no idea what The Haven of Rest Rescue Mission was or why people went there. Since I did not know what I was getting myself into, I was determined to be careful and observant. We pulled in the parking lot of an impressive brick building in downtown Akron. The interior was modern, spotless clean and very nice. It was an attractive building inside and outside. People were mingling, talking and laughing in the lobby; it seemed they were happy to be there. Several of them greeted us warmly, and welcomed us with smiles. They did not even know us, yet they were pleased to see us.

It was time for the chapel service. As we followed the crowd into the chapel, I speculated, was this some kind of a church? My mind processed and analyzed everything. I noticed all the people who came to this meeting walked up toward the front of the room. We passed by several rows of men sitting toward the rear of the room, poorly dressed, shabby, a pathetic mass of humanity. Who were they? Could it be, they were the ones they rescued or tried to rescue? From what? All too soon, I had to put my questions aside; the service had started.

A tall, gracious man with a kind face stood by the platform at the front. He greeted and welcomed everyone. This service, or meeting, had a friendly relaxed atmosphere. If this was a church service, it was unlike any I had ever experienced. The entire group, with radiant faces, was singing songs I never heard before. I tried to follow the words in the book, "Marvelous grace of our loving Lord, Grace that exceeds our sin and our guilt"....moreover, "this grace will pardon and cleanse from sin." Before I could translate and understand its meaning, they were singing about "rescuing the perishing because Jesus was merciful." Where was I? What was this place all about? While the songs were in English, I still could not understand their meaning.

The gracious man asked the group to recite a verse from the Bible, John 3:16. In unison, they recited, "For God so loved the world that He gave His only begotten Son, that whoever believes in Him should not perish but have everlasting life." Could this be true? God loved the world? The gracious man said many things that evening that made me think. All this was too new, too good to be true. It was too simple, there had to be more to it than God loved the world. I could not ponder his statements for long because he announced it was "Testimony Time." Before I could comprehend what that meant, people stood up all over that room, talking about this God who loved them. God, who by His grace, saved them from addictions and horrible lifestyles. Because of Him, many were reunited with their families and children. God reached down into the depths of sin, rescued them, and made them whole.

All these things were so new, so different from anything I had ever heard, yet, I was skeptical, there had to be some catch to this. I yearned to know more, but I had been disappointed by religions before and I would not let that happen again.

In my room that evening, I searched my Bible for this John 3:16, I wanted to read it again. I found it, read it, and re-read it. Once started, I read other verses around it and then finished the entire book of John that evening. Every evening I would read other chapters of the New Testament, but I always returned to the Psalms. I wanted to know, if this was for real, why didn't other people talk about it?

I decided I would attend this "church" and I looked forward to the Haven of Rest on Saturday nights. I learned the name of the gracious man, who conducted the services, was none other than the Reverend C. C. Thomas, the founder of the Haven of Rest Ministries. The Haven was, and is, a faith based Christian ministry uncompromisingly committed to glorifying God. Through a Christ-centered outreach of love and compassion, the Haven of Rest served the physical, emotional and spiritual needs of all those who entered through its doors without regard to race, color, creed or social standing.

ENCOUNTER WITH JESUS CHRIST

I was a very private person; I could not talk about my feelings, and from hard experience, I learned to keep things to myself. I did not have a closed mind. I truly wanted to know about forgiveness and this gift of a new life that is offered to those who trust in Jesus Christ. Nevertheless, I was confused; after all, we were not heathens, we lived in a civilized society, weren't we all Christians?

I had an analytical mind, I was not a skeptic, I needed to know and wanted to know. I had many questions and conflicts that I was examining and trying to resolve as I attended Saturday night after Saturday night. Much to my surprise as the Saturdays passed; many of my questions would be answered without my asking.

What about all those rules that I could not even remember, let alone keep? What about good deeds? All religions demand that we perform some sort of penance, do good deeds to find favor with God. But, if we are all sinners, how could we do good deeds? In Romans 3:23 it states, "for all have sinned and come short of the glory of God." I had no problem accepting it; I knew that since childhood. What was I supposed to do about it? I helped others, I tried to be good. Yet, I did not know if God would consider them good deeds, or even when I did enough of them. I found the answer in Ephesians 2:8, "For by grace you have been saved through faith, and that not of yourselves; it is the gift of God, not of works, lest any man should boast." A gift, amazing! I knew that a gift is a generous act on the part of the giver. I could accept it or reject it, but I could not buy it or it would not be a gift.

What about my sins? God is holy, how could I approach Him if He does not allow sinful people into His presence? I John 1:9 gave me the answer, "If we confess our sins, He is faithful and just to forgive us our sins and to cleanse us from all unrighteousness." All because God so loved that He gave His only Son, the Lord Jesus Christ, not me, Jesus did it all, out of His amazing love for me. "If you confess with your mouth the Lord Jesus and believe in your heart that God has raised Him from the dead, you will be saved. For with the heart one believes to righteousness, and with the mouth confession is made to salvation" (Romans 10:9–10).

Throughout my life, God, by His grace, used events, circumstances, and people to bring me to a place called Haven of Rest where I encountered the Sovereign of the universe, the almighty, holy God, whom I feared as long as I could remember. There, He revealed His character, His divine nature, and His unfailing love to my seeking heart. I experienced His liberating love, love that heals a broken and longing heart. Love beyond comprehension. Love poured out on Cavalry's cross. Yes, He is a God of justice, but also a God of unconditional love.

Praise God there was room at the cross for me. For upon that cross Jesus took my place, the pure sinless Son of God gave His life so I could be forgiven. He died so I could live. Hallelujah! What a Savior! I left all the pain, all the hurt, all the hate at the foot of His cross. I embraced my new life in Christ. My soul found rest in His unconditional love. Freedom that begins at the cross gives joy and celebrates life. "If anyone is in Christ, he is a new creation, old things have passed away; behold all things have become new" (2 Corinthians 5:17).

Freedom, throughout the ages, has been precious to those who endured the bondage of tyranny. Countless numbers had given their all to secure freedom for themselves, their fellowmen, or their nation and to gain political freedom, to live as free man with dignity. Nevertheless, there is a freedom that is more precious than anything we can experience or attain even in a democracy. This freedom is not free nor is it cheap. This freedom was purchased for all men by the precious blood of Jesus Christ sacrificed on Calvary's cross. Forgiveness and pardon is God's gracious gift to all. This freedom sets us free so we can fulfill our God given destiny.

"And you shall know the truth, and the truth shall make you free. Therefore if the Son makes you free, you shall be free indeed" (John 8:32, 36).

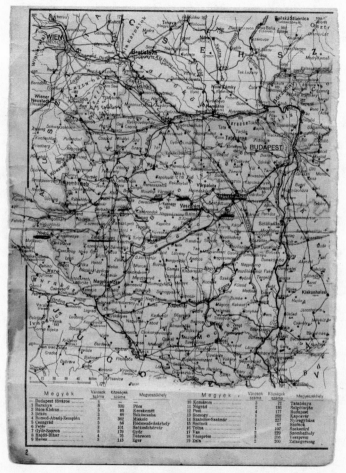

Escape Route, 1957

Author, age 15 at the time of escape

Csepregi Family home early 1900

Uncle Marton

Father, Francis Csepregi, 1943

Mother, Julianna Csepregi, 1940

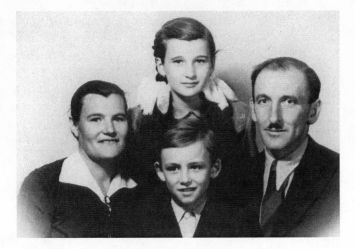

Family photo, 1953